MAKING
LEATHER
HANDBAGS

© 2004 by Quarry Books

First published in the United States of America by
Quarry Books, an imprint of
Rockport Publishers, Inc.
33 Commercial Street
Gloucester, Massachusetts 01930-5089
Telephone: (978) 282-9590
Fax: (978) 283-2742
www.rockpub.com

Library of Congress Cataloging-in-Publication Data
Goldstein-Lynch, Ellen.
   Making leather handbags and other stylish accessories / Ellen Goldstein-Lynch, Sarah Mullins, Nicole Malone.
      p.   cm.
   ISBN 1-59253-076-1 (pbk.)
   1. Handbags. 2. Leatherwork. I. Mullins, Sarah. II. Malone, Nicole. III. Title.
TT667.G6523 2004
745.53'1—dc22   2004006841
                                                                                    CIP

ISBN 1-59253-076-1

10 9 8 7 6 5 4 3 2 1

Design: Dutton & Sherman Design
Cover Design: Jean DeBenedictis
Photography: BeeDigital/Bruce Myren
Step Illustrations: Judy Love
Pattern Illustrations: Roberta Frauwirth

Printed in China

MAKING LEATHER HANDBAGS

AND OTHER STYLISH ACCESSORIES

GLOUCESTER MASSACHUSETTS

QUARRY BOOKS

Ellen Goldstein-Lynch, Sarah Mullins, Nicole Malone
of the Accessories Design Department at the Fashion Institute of Technology, NYC

contents

introduction

Something happens to our emotional state every time we pick up a leather handbag or small leather accessory. Maybe it's the image of our leather accessories being carefully made in a small European factory by talented craftsmen who work by candlelight into the wee hours of the morning, or maybe it's the feel of softness against our hand, or the smell of leather itself. Whatever the reason, a smile crosses our face, and we find that we can't get enough of them.

From the Stone Age to the present day, women and men have fawned over leather accessories. Handbags made by Gucci, Ferragamo, Fendi, Prada, and Coach put most people in a trancelike state. In the stores you can always find these accessories behind glass or on display pedestals, making them special and just a tad out of reach. These accessories are in a class by themselves, the crème de la crème. Buying one has always been a thrill, whether or not the style, color, or shape suited our needs. After all, these accessories are made by masters.

But what if you want something a little different, something affordable and functional that suits *your* needs exactly? You'd have to comb the stores looking for just the right piece—an affordable leather accessory that is styled just the right way, with the right type of leather, in the perfect shade and size and, oh yes, with the appropriate number of compartments. If you ever did manage to find that bag, it would be virtually impossible to coordinate all the small leather goods you need into it. Whether it is a cosmetic bag, a cell phone holder, a wallet, an eyeglasses case, or an agenda book, most small leather accessories come in basic shapes and colors, with little or no personality. Don't worry. This book is the answer to just such dilemmas.

Making Leather Handbags and Other Stylish Accessories—the follow-up to our first book, *Making Handbags*—offers you, the home sewer or leather craft enthusiast, the opportunity to create fashion-forward, trendy, stylish, and elegant handbags and small fashion accessories in your favorite material—leather.

This book allows you to be as creative as your imagination permits by incorporating your choice of leathers, embellishments, trims, and techniques to create your own one-of-a-kind designs. We also provide you with patterns for making stylized personal accessories that you can coordinate to your newly designed handbags. It's time you left the leather masters' designs on the shelf and the mass-market handbag and accessory styles in the stores. Start creating your own unique and original designs, made by you with you in mind.

Making Leather Handbags and Other Stylish Accessories is your ticket to making professional leather accessories. So, get your studio space in order, set aside some time to work, make sure your sewing machine is operational, and get those design juices flowing—your future accessories wardrobe awaits. And it just may become the talk of the town.

SECTION ONE

getting started

FASHION AND STYLING:
IT'S IN THE BAG—FASHION OR NOT, YOU CHOOSE!

There has never been a time when women have just bought a handbag without thinking what they were going to put into it. When you think about it, this train of thought is logical. If the handbag is small, we assume that we can put only a small wallet, a cell phone, and a credit card holder into it. On the other hand, if we have a larger bag, we can put everything in it, including the kitchen sink, and not even think twice. The only problem is the weight of the bag. So, we carry more than one bag. Our day bag houses all the small fashion accessories, and our tote bag is filled with more functional items, such as a cosmetic bag, an agenda book, or a second pair of eyeglasses.

Men are different. Up until recently, men relied heavily on their wives, girlfriends, or companions to carry their eyeglasses, cell phones, or even wallets. Now men are more apt to carry their cell phone on a belt, their wallet in their back or breast pocket, and their agenda book or handheld computer in their briefcase.

In most cases, personal leather goods and small fashion accessories come in basic shapes, are made in traditional colors and materials, and are sold separately in the store, boutique, or catalog. These items historically have lacked the fashion forwardness and trendiness that handbags have. Both men and women have settled for what has been available. If they wanted to coordinate their small fashion accessories that meant all black, all red, or all brown. It didn't mean all red alligator or all black lizard.

Now you can break out of the traditional mold of small fashion accessories and coordinate them to what ever your handbag designs might be. Even if it's a teal blue envelope bag with orange snakeskin trim, now you can make your agenda book, eyeglasses case, and wallet mimic that same silhouette. For the very first time, your small fashion accessories can match your personality, your outfit, and your favorite handbag.

Men and women have a choice to be different and distinct in their handbags as well as their small fashion accessories. The decision is yours: You can either follow the pack or be the leader. All it takes is a conscientious effort to be creative. It's all about being fashionable.

SUPPLIES AND TOOLS

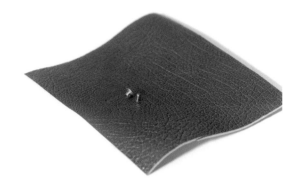

A ASSEMBLE MATERIALS AND PUNCH HOLE.

B PLACE RIVET POST THROUGH HOLE, PUSH RIVET CAP ON TO POST, HAMMER RIVET SETTER OVER CAP TO SET.

C REMOVE SETTER AND CHECK THAT RIVET IS SECURELY SET.

No one says that you need to have a fully equipped sewing room or studio to make handbags and small fashion accessories. All you need are a few basics and, of course, your imagination.

You definitely need a **sewing machine**—the specific type doesn't matter, as long as you are comfortable working with it. The machine should have an automatic *reverse-stitch selector* and *interchangeable pressor foot attachments*. Some of the best machines are the old Singer treadles, but the newer models work just as well. You can also use the machines with a computer memory for embroidery and embellishment detailing as well as regular sewing. Although most projects featured in this book can be completed on a home sewing machine, if you want to purchase a commercial sewing machine, these machines are available for home use. Just make sure that whatever machine you do use is well oiled and maintained. A sluggish machine is a hungry machine and will tend to "eat" your material.

Pressor-foot attachments are available for most machines. Think in terms of zipper, gauge, and binding attachments. Teflon ones are appropriate for working on leather and suede, and will fit most home sewing machines. Do your homework, and make the investment. You never know when your imagination will call on your "feet" to do the work.

Find a **flat surface** to work on. A folding table, kitchen table, or sewing table is perfect. Make sure the table is secure and not wobbly. Also make sure that the surface is clean. You don't want food, grease, or grime to get on your projects.

When cutting leather, be sure to use a **cutting board**. The board not only protects your table, but also provides a stable surface for cutting. Many boards are "self healing," which means they mend any cut marks themselves. Just make sure that the cutting board you use has a smooth surface.

A NEEDLE-NOSE PLIERS

B MALLET

C HAMMER

D ROTARY CUTTER

E METAL RULER

F ROTARY HOLE PUNCH

G 69 NYLON THREAD

H RIVET AND SNAP SETTER KIT

I TOP: GAUGE FOOT, MIDDLE: TEFLON FOOT, BOTTOM: ZIPPER FOOT

J HOLE PUNCH

K OVAL PUNCH

L RIVET SETTER

M BINDER CLIPS

N GROMMET SETTER

O AWL

P BONE FOLDER

Q CRAFT KNIFE

R SEAM RIPPER

S MAGNETIC SNAP AND WASHERS

T TURN LOCK

U BUCKLE

V D RING, O RING

W GROMMET AND WASHER

X RIVET

Y COLLAR PIN SET

PUNCHING A HOLE

PLACE THE PUNCH OVER THE LEATHER AND HIT WITH MALLET.

Lighting is critical. Without proper lighting your eyes will play tricks on you. Natural light is the best, but if you don't have that don't worry. Just make sure you have sufficient light when sewing.

When using craft or fabric glue, be sure to work near a window or with a fan on, to ensure **proper ventilation**. If you start to get a headache from the glue, stop working immediately and get some fresh air.

Rubber cement, also known as **contact cement,** is essential for all leather handbag and fashion accessories projects. When working with two pieces of leather or suede, you need to cement both pieces, let the cement dry, and then put the pieces together. Before getting started, though, make sure your cement is relatively new (less than six months old), read the instructions for using it (Is proper ventilation needed?), and have an extra jar available just in case. Also, be sure to use newspaper on your gluing surface to prevent excess glue from getting onto your table and, ultimately, onto your project. Remember: When you are cementing on suede, be as neat as you can because cement does not rub off suede.

You will need a **good, reliable iron** for getting wrinkles out of fabric linings, securing fusible interfacing, and creasing some of the leathers. Just keep in mind that although you can use steam on fabric, *you should not use steam on leather or suede.*

A craftsperson can never have too many pairs of **scissors**. Just make sure they are sharp enough to cut through leather. You may even want to have one pair reserved strictly for cutting leather and another strictly for fabric. Also important is that the scissors fit comfortably in your hand. Various ergonomically correct scissors are on the market, so do your homework and shop around. A **rotary cutter** is also great for cutting both leather and fabric, so make sure you have one of those in your sewing box as well.

A AFTER HOLE IS PUNCHED, PLACE GROMMET THROUGH THE HOLE FROM THE FRONT. PLACE GROMMET ON THE ANVIL FRONT-SIDE DOWN. PLACE WASHER OVER GROMMET ON THE BACK SIDE.

B PLACE SETTER INTO THE GROMMET AND HIT WITH MALLET.

C REMOVE SETTER AND CHECK THAT RIVET IS SECURELY SET.

Pinking shears are great for decorative detailing, but make sure they are sharp. Dull pinking shears won't even cut butter.

Utility and craft knives are ideal for cutting leather. Again, just make sure the blade is sharp.

To get a smooth folded edge on leather, you need to use a **bone folder**. The original bone folders were made of whalebone, but the newer models are made of plastic. Also, some bone folders are strictly for left- or right-handed people. Just be sure to get the one that's right for you. Check your craft catalogs and resource lists for more information.

We recommend that you use a strong **thread,** whichever type works best on your machine. Nylon thread works well with leather and suede, so you might want to consider using it. For some projects you'll need contrasting colors, so stock up on your favorites. Also, remember to buy embroidery thread for adding contrasting details to your projects; you can use either pearl cotton or embroidery floss.

Most machines do come with **needles**, and in some cases you can buy a variety pack. Just make sure that you have a range of different sizes for stitching different fabrics and that you invest in leather needles for sewing different weights of leather and suede.

Hand-sewing needles are also essential, so make sure you have a variety of those on hand as well. If you are going to be doing embroidery, use an **embroidery needle**. For beading on leather, use a **glover's needle**; for lacing on leather, use a **lacing needle**. Just remember to change your needles regularly. Like scissors, they tend to get dull with repeated use.

You'll need **straight pins** for pinning lining and fabric in place. Whether you buy them on a wheel or in a box, just

ADDING A COLLAR PIN

A AFTER PUNCHING A HOLE, PLACE THE SCREW THROUGH THE HOLE FROM THE BOTTOM.

B SCREW COLLAR PIN ON.

make sure you have enough on hand. Also remember that you can't use straight pins on leather or suede because they will leave marks.

Binder, or **bulldog, clips** are those black metal clips used to hold papers together. They are also great for holding several pieces of leather together, making the sewing process a lot easier. They're like having an extra pair of hands. The ¾" to 1" (1.9 cm to 2.5 cm) size is perfect for most projects. You can buy them individually or in packages, in black or in a variety of colors at office supply stores.

Double-sided craft tape is great for turning in edges of fabric or leather. It's also perfect for temporarily adhering pieces before sewing, rather than using glue and risk having it seep into the fabric or leather and staining it. The ¼" (5 mm) size is the best to use.

Masking tape, that "old reliable," comes in handy for almost any craft project, especially for holding the leather in place while you cut out your patterns. Keep several rolls on hand.

Metal rulers are the best type of ruler to use when working with leather and suede. You get a more accurate cut when you use them to guide your cutting, and in the long run, they will save your fingers.

Snap-, grommet-, eyelet-, and **rivet-setting kits** along with a **rotary** or **handheld leather hole punch** are also important for leather and suede projects. Snaps, grommets, and rivets add decorative pizzazz to your designs and really jazz up a collection, and a rotary punch makes it easier to make holes in the leather. If you're a serious craftsperson, you need these items in your supply inventory.

USING A LEATHER PUNCH

A PLACE OVAL PUNCH IN DESIRED LOCATION AND HIT WITH MALLET.

B REMOVE PUNCH.

For making holes in patterns and in your leather, you will need a really sharp **awl**. It looks like an old-fashioned ice pick with a wooden bulbous handle. The craftsperson's version has a fine point, which is perfect for these projects. Wider points, on the other hand, are not effective in penetrating patterns or leather. You can buy an awl in a craft store, through a catalog, or at a hardware store.

Also, don't forget to have an ample supply of **fabric-marking pens and pencils** and **silver pens** on hand for transferring pattern pieces onto your fabric, leather, or suede.

Other optional tools that can make crafting life easier are a pair of **needle-nose pliers**, a **handsaw**, and a rawhide **mallet** or **hammer**. In the back of this book you will find an extensive resource list of suppliers of materials and tools. We suggest that you refer to this section when you are updating your supply inventory. Many of the resources have websites and catalogs.

With the recommended list of supplies in hand, you are now equipped with the crafting essentials necessary for creating the leather projects in this book. So, what are you waiting for? Grab your supplies, label them, and put them in handy carriers or in an easily accessible place. Make sure that the tools are sharpened, your machine is well oiled, and the pieces to your kits are all there. Before you start on that first project, though, check out the chapter, the ABCs of Leather.

THE ABCS OF LEATHER

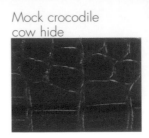

Mock crocodile
cow hide

Printed hair-on
calf skin

You are now officially ready to take the design plunge. You've picked out your pattern, and you have ideas floating around in your head. However, before you venture out to the stores or turn to your favorite leather resource catalog for supplies, you will want to keep in mind some important guidelines regarding the purchasing of leather. As one famous retailer claims, "an educated consumer is our best customer!" When it comes to leathers, understanding the language and how to buy them, makes you an educated, confident consumer.

The first thing you need to know is whether the leather you are buying is a **hide** or a **skin**. The easiest way to remember the difference is by size. Larger animals, such as *cow*, *buffalo*, and *deer*, are hides. Because of the size of the animal, the hide is usually cut in half and sold as sides for handbags and footwear. In some countries, the hide is cut into smaller pieces, referred to as shoulder, back, and belly. Smaller animals, such as *calf*, *goat*, *pig*, and *snake*, are referred to as skins because you buy the whole animal.

Next you need to know which type of leather will be suitable for your design project. For most of the designs featured in this book, *cow*, *calf*, *goat*, or *kid* are your best choices. These leathers are the easiest to sew. They maintain their shape better than other leathers and are easy to manipulate. Whatever you do, stay away from *patent leather*. Patent leather, because of its finish, is probably one of the most difficult leathers to work with.

If you are interested in using **hand-tooling** techniques or **decorative painting** on your leather, stick with leather that does not have a finish. In most stores or catalogs, this type of leather is referred to as "vegetable tanned" or "tooling" leather.

Suede is a finish that is added to the hide or skin to create a buffed or brushed surface.

Embossed leather features a pattern on the surface of the hide or skin. Embossing is generally used to simulate other, more expensive animal skins, such as alligator and crocodile.

Silk-screened leather has a design motif that has been added to the surface of the skin.

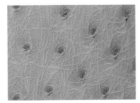

Ostrich skin

Woven embossed
cow hide

Nubuck

Pebble grain
cow hide

Python skin Pig skin Silk-screen printed pig suede Calf skin

Hair-on leather offers another type of finish. During the tanning process, the hair is left on and finished to simulate pony, zebra, tiger, or other animal skins. If you intend to use this type of cowhide, make sure the hair is short. This particular type of leather is difficult to manipulate for sewn bags. However, if you are using it for raw-edge designs with hand-lacing techniques, it is perfect.

Leather is sold in square feet, and its thickness is measured in ounces. If you are doing raw-edge or laced treatments, go with a thicker leather (4 to 7 oz.). If your designs call for turned-in edges, use thinner leather (1 to 3 oz.). Thinner leathers have a better hand and are easier to manipulate.

Leather, like other natural materials, is subject to imperfections. You will find stretch marks, scarring, and brand markings on the surface of the skin. Make sure the leather you select is appropriate for your design project. The leather should have the right degree of manipulation. In other words, a heavier or stiffer hand would be appropriate for a raw-edge design, whereas a more pliable hand would produce a softer product.

When it comes to adding creativity to your projects, think **exotic leathers. Snakeskin** used as an appliqué or decorative motif can accentuate your finished design. When used properly, snakeskin or other exotic leathers can add a touch of sophistication, thereby creating your one-of-a-kind design.

Now you're armed and ready to shop for your leather supplies. However, before you walk out your door or turn on your computer, remember your ABCs:

- **A**sk questions about the leather you are purchasing.
- **B**e knowledgeable of the leather terminology.
- **C**heck to make sure that the leather looks right and smells right, and that it doesn't have too many imperfections.

Remember: If you're not completely satisfied with the hide or skin, don't buy it.

 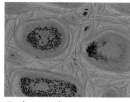  

Embossed cow hide Embossed patent cow hide Lizagator embossed cow hide Metallic patent cow hide

EMBELLISHMENTS AND TRIMS

Embellishments can either make or break your design. They add character to your creation. They express you and your personality. They are what separate your design from anyone else's. What's more, they tie your collection of accessories together, making them special and unique.

Selecting the right type of trim or embellishment is up to you. Whatever suits your mood, your outfit, and your attitude is ultimately the right one to use. So, in keeping with that adage that change is good, here are a few trims and embellishments that can add character to your creations.

APPLIQUÉ

Appliqués come in various colors, sizes, and shapes. Embroidered patches, flowers, initials, and animals all make great additions to the outside of your handbags and small fashion accessories. You will find that pieces of snakeskin and surface appliqués of initials on leather also make a striking statement.

While we're talking appliqué, don't forget **reverse appliqué**, which adds color and shape through cutwork. This type of appliqué gives your design a personality all its own. Remember to experiment with exotic skins for appliqué. They are a major plus in this category of trims and embellishments!

Trapunto can help give your collection a three-dimensional look. This effect is created by padding your design motif. By topstitching your designs with contrasting threads, you can add a touch of whimsy or

stylish sophistication to a small fashion accessory or handbag silhouette.

You can never have enough **baubles, bangles,** and **beads,** especially when you look at all the beaded embellishments on the bags in the stores. They come in various colors, sizes, and shapes, and can be hand sewn to the leather or suede using a *glover's needle*. If it's gemstones you're looking to add, purchase a *Be-Dazzler Stud & Rhinestone Setter* or a *stone-setting kit*. Whatever you choose, choose it wisely. You're creating a fashion statement that just may make your designs the talk of the neighborhood.

Buttons are used as closures as well as embellishments. They come in various colors, shapes, and sizes, so you can search for just the right ones for your projects. Also, remember that some catalogs and stores specialize in antique and collectible buttons, if that's what you're into.

Embroidery stitches such as satin, French knot, couch, and leaf stitches are just a few of the types of stitches you can use to add dimension and interest to your projects. Use these decorative stitches by themselves or with embroidery appliqués for added impact. Just remember that when applying this technique to leather or suede you need to use an embroidery needle.

Flowers for that straight-from-the-garden look can be found in silk. Use one as a focal point on the flap of a bag or handle. Shop for just the right one. Most craft stores have a huge garden blooming year-round.

Fringe and **tassels** make amazing trims because they are three-dimensional and add movement. So, if

Topstitch

Lacing

Button

Piping

you're looking for that special something that catches people's eyes when you walk, consider adding a little bit of fringe or a tassel. Just remember not to overdo it so much that it gets in your way.

GROMMETS

Grommets, eyelets, snaps, and **studs**, besides serving as functional embellishments, can also be used as trims. Cover the entire front of the bag or small fashion accessory with grommets and eyelets for a military look. Use snaps to attach appliqués to your collection so you can change the appliqué with your outfit. Studs are fabulous for making that urban statement really stand out.

JEWELRY

Use old pieces of **jewelry**, such as necklaces and pins, to accent your collections. These can be either permanently affixed or changed with your outfit. It's always fun to go scavenging through flea markets and antique stores for just the right piece. Also, don't forget that necklaces and bracelets make great handles as well.

Lace and **lace appliqué** add sophistication and worldliness to any creation. Whether you use lace pieces, small Battenberg flowers, or ruffled lace stripes, the end result is breathtakingly elegant.

Lacing is a technique that works beautifully on raw-edge leather and suede projects. It adds an urban or rustic look that is perfect for the fashion-current designer.

And let's not forget about **leather tooling**. Here is your opportunity to go wide with design and motifs. Select the right type of leather (either vegetable-tanned or tooling leather) and always experiment with a small piece first. There are many catalogs that feature tooling equipment, so shop for just the right ones.

Use **fabric paint, acrylic paint**, or **luma dyes** to add a bit of whimsy to your bags and small fashion accessories. Experiment with a small piece of leather first to make sure that the paint doesn't crack or peel.

Although **quilting** and **smocking** are techniques rather than trims, they can be used to enhance your collection "three-dimensionally." Again, experiment with the techniques before using them on your designs. You might consider smocking a flap or quilting a pocket for greater design impact.

Decorative ribbons can create a three-dimensional effect that separates your creations from others. Use ribbons as part of your embroidery, creating flowers or leaves on pockets, flaps, or handles.

Go shopping at the hardware store and in thrift shops for different and interesting pieces of **hardware** to attach to your creations. Consider decorative drawer pulls for handles, wooden knobs and dowels, or even some funky metal tubing and washers. You never know what you will find. A hardware store is like a treasure trove of interesting finds, so use your imagination.

Topstitching, like embroidery stitching, adds detail to your creations. Use a contrasting color of thread when topstitching, as we did on the Envelope Bag (page 32).

LAYING OUT AND CUTTING YOUR PATTERNS AND SEWING

You've just come back from your leather-buying spree with the most fabulous colors and skins. You've decided on the first project, and you've coordinated your purchases to that favorite dress hanging in your closet. Before you do anything, you need to follow your ABCs, but this time they mean something different. This time we're talking about how to lay out and cut your patterns and sew:

A—Be acutely aware of any imperfections in the leather you are using. Such imperfections could be the result of a barbwire scratch, a brand mark, or even stretch marks. Yes, even animals have a tendency to fluctuate in weight. When positioning your patterns, use the areas with the fewest imperfections.

B—Back, belly, and shoulder portions of the hide are the best areas to use. When placing your patterns, use as much of the best areas of the hide as possible, especially for the front and the back of the project. You can use the "less attractive" areas for piping, bottoms, and handle linings. Avoid using sides and edges of the skin, if possible, because they provide the least amount of durability. By keeping your pattern placement controlled, you stand a better chance of using the rest of the hide for those other projects, such as a cell phone holder or an eyeglasses case. Just remember, before you cut, make sure all pattern pieces are in the right place.

C—Check to make sure that your tabletop is covered with a cutting board or cutting surface. This prevents you from ruining your table.

D—When cutting out patterns, don't cut the leather with scissors. Instead use a utility or craft knife and use a straightedge for cutting straight edges. A metal ruler is the perfect solution. When cutting around curved edges, use the pattern as your guide.

E—Be extra careful when using tape to hold your patterns down on the leather. Test the leather first. Some tapes may remove the finish from the leather and leave a mark.

Congratulations, you have graduated leather class. You know what types of leather are available, how to lay out patterns, where to cut, and how to cut. You've checked and rechecked that all pattern pieces are correctly placed before you cut. You've tested your tape, sharpened your knife, and secured a metal ruler. There's just one more area you haven't mastered yet and that's sewing. The letters F and G tell you how.

F—Using a Teflon foot for your leather projects can and will be a lifesaver. The Teflon coating allows the leather to move effortlessly through the feeder portion of the machine. Although you can sew leather without a Teflon foot, why make your sewing experience difficult? Teflon foot attachments are available at most sewing supply stores and fit most home sewing machines. And, while we're talking about "feet," let's not forget the letter G.

G—A gauge foot can act as your sewing guide: It allows you to sew in a straight line without causing your leather or material to pucker or waiver. A zipper foot, on the other hand, allows you to sew close to zipper teeth or piping.

Now it's on to the wonderful world of leather handbags and small fashion accessories— or, better yet, the realm of your imagination!

NOTES: For additional help with specific sewing terms see the Glossary on page 123. For information on leather supplies, tools, and notations, see Resources on page 124.

SECTION TWO

projects

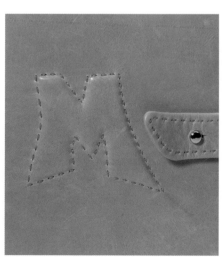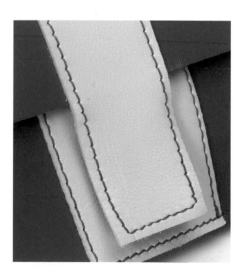

tote bag

The tote bag is probably *the* most versatile bag in a woman's wardrobe. Whether it's large or small, made of leather or fabric, this bag goes from home to office in style! Our tote is made of rugged-looking distressed leather, with contrasting decorative corners, coordinated flap, and a turn-lock closure. The handles are attached with grommets for a more sophisticated appearance. This smart tote also sports punched and pinked detailing on both the corners and the closure. This tote is the ultimate accessory for kicking back on a weekend excursion or for carrying all your necessities to work in style.

MATERIALS
- 5 square feet (0.5 sq. m) of 2 to 3 oz. leather for outside
- 1½ square feet (0.1 sq. m) of 2 to 3 oz. leather for appliqué
- 12¾" × 3" (32 cm × 7.5 cm) of stiffened felt
- ¼ yard (23 cm) of lining fabric
- ¼ yard (23 cm) of medium-weight Pellon interfacing
- Six ¼" (5 mm) long rivets
- Four ½" (1.3 cm) grommets
- 1 turn-lock closure with plate
- Matching thread for machine sewing
- Rubber cement

TOOLS
- Rotary or handheld leather hole punch, size #2
- ½" (1.3 cm) handheld punch
- Rivet-setting kit
- Grommet-setting kit
- Utility or craft knife
- Pinking shears
- Needle-nose pliers
- Iron
- Awl
- Bone folder
- 12" (30.5 cm) and 24" (61 cm) metal rulers
- Masking tape and/or pattern weights
- Binder clips
- Scissors
- Rawhide mallet or hammer
- Fabric-marking pencil
- Cardboard, 8 oz. leather, or wood for punching board

MACHINERY
Home sewing machine with leather needle, gauge foot, zipper foot, and Teflon foot

GETTING STARTED
Cut out all leather and fabric pieces from the tote bag patterns, following the instructions on the patterns. All leather pieces should be cut out separately.

When cutting leather or materials for patterns, either loop masking tape onto the back of the patterns or use pattern weights to keep patterns in place while cutting. *Note: Always test leather before using masking tape to hold down your pattern. Masking tape may remove the finish from the leather or leave a mark on it.*

Line up the metal ruler along the straight edges of the patterns, and cut the leather with the utility or craft knife. Let the edge of the ruler guide the knife as you cut. When cutting rounded edges, simply use the edge of your pattern as a guide. *Note: Be sure to cut on a proper surface.*

Use a fabric-marking pencil to trace patterns onto the lining fabric and Pellon, and cut out the pieces with scissors. Transfer the pocket placement onto one piece of the lining.

SPECIAL CUTTING INSTRUCTIONS
Cut out four pieces of outside leather, each measuring 1" × 24" (2.5 cm × 61 cm). Rubber cement the pieces with the flesh sides together to create two 1" × 24" (2.5 cm × 61 cm) strips. Use the handle pattern to cut the pieces to the correct width. Transfer the hole placements for the rivets.

Repeat the same steps for the tab pieces, cutting the strips 10" × 3" (25.5 × 7.5 cm), cementing them together, and cutting them to size using the pattern.

Cut out the appliqué pieces from the corner and tab patterns. Transfer the hole markings for the decorative holes as labeled on the patterns, and punch the holes using the leather hole punch. Use pinking shears to cut the curved edges of the corners and all around the tab piece. Transfer the hole placements for the turn-lock closure and rivets onto the tab appliqué.

STEP 1

Rubber cement around the edges on the flesh side of the front and back leather pieces and around the Pellon. Adhere the Pellon to the flesh side of the leather ³⁄₈" (1 cm) below the top edge. If the Pellon extends beyond the leather edge, trim the Pellon.

STEP 2

Rubber cement the top edge of the leather and the Pellon. Fold the top ³⁄₈" (1 cm) edge of the leather onto the Pellon.

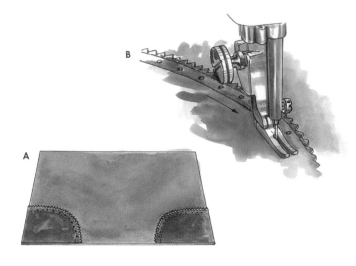

STEP 3

Rubber cement the flesh side of the corner appliqué pieces, and adhere them to the corners of the front and back leather pieces, as noted on the pattern (A). Topstitch the appliqué corners onto the front and back leather pieces with two rows of stitches on either side of the decorative holes (B).

STEP 5

STEP 4

Punch the holes for the rivets in the outside back leather piece, as noted on the pattern. Cut the prong slots for the turn-lock closure in the outside front leather piece, as noted on the pattern. *Remember: Turn lock closures vary in size, so be sure to cut the hole and prong slots to match your lock.*

STEP 5

Rubber cement the flesh side of the bottom leather piece and the stiffened felt. Adhere the felt to the leather, centering the felt so there is ³⁄₈" (1 cm) of leather all around the felt. Rubber cement the two long edges of the leather and felt, and then fold the edges of leather onto the felt.

STEP 6

Rubber cement the bottom onto the outside front leather piece. Be sure the bottom is centered from left to right and overlaps the front piece by ³⁄₈" (1 cm). Topstitch the bottom onto the front leather piece ¹⁄₈" (3 mm) from the edge using a gauge foot or a Teflon foot. Begin and end by back tacking the topstitch ³⁄₈" (1 cm) from the short ends of the bottom.

STEP 7

Repeat Step 6 to attach the bottom to the outside back piece.

STEP 8

Fold the outside front and back pieces with the right sides together, lining up the top edges. Stitch each side seam together using ³⁄₈" (1 cm) seam allowance, back tacking at the beginning and end of the seam.

STEP 6

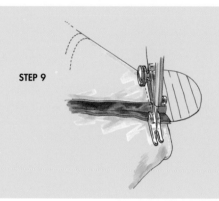

STEP 9

STEP 9

To create the flat bottom, pull the side seam open and the bottom edges into the corners of the seam. With the right sides together, stitch across the opening using ³⁄₈" (1 cm) seam allowance, back tacking at the beginning and end of the seam. This seam will be perpendicular to the side seam.

STEP 10

Repeat Step 9 for the other bottom edge.

STEP 11

Rubber cement the tab appliqué piece onto the outside leather tab pieces. Topstitch around the tab with two rows of stitches on either side of the decorative holes.

STEP 12

Punch the two holes for the rivets through the tab, as noted on the tab pattern, using a #2 punch. Cut the hole and the prong slots through the tab for the turn lock closure, as noted on the tab pattern, using a utility or craft knife. *Remember: Turn-lock closures vary in size, so be sure to cut the hole and prong slots to match your lock.*

STEP 13

Place turn-lock through the tab, and fold the prongs onto the washer using needle-nose pliers. Rivet the tab to the outside back piece using a rivet-setting kit.

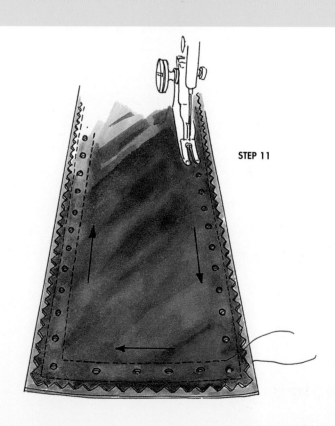

STEP 11

STEP 14
Prepare the lining pocket by folding over the three sides, as noted on the pattern. Use an iron to press the sides down. Then fold and press the pocket on the centerline, as noted on the pattern. *The bottom, back edge of the pocket is raw and should be ⅛" (3 mm) shorter than the front to reduce bulk.*

STEP 15
Pin the pocket onto the lining, as noted on the lining front and back patterns, with the center fold as the opening. Topstitch around the side and bottom edges of the pocket ⅛" (3 mm) from the edge using a gauge foot.

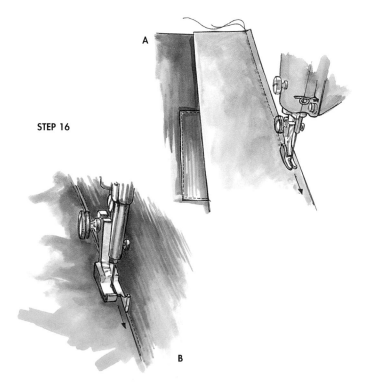

STEP 16
Stitch the lining collar to the top edge of the lining front piece with the right sides together using ⅜" (1 cm) seam allowance (A). Fold the collar open, and topstitch along the bottom edge of the leather collar ⅛" (3 mm) from the edge using a gauge foot (B).

STEP 17
Repeat Step 16 to attach the other lining collar to the lining back piece.

STEP 18
Pin the front and back lining pieces together with right sides together. Stitch down the side seams and across the bottom using ⅜" (1 cm) seam allowance, back tacking at the beginning and end of the seam.

STEP 19

Press open the side and bottom seams. With right sides together, match the side and bottom seams and stitch across the opening using ³/₈" (1 cm) seam allowance, back tacking at the beginning and end of the seam. The bottom seam will be perpendicular to the side seams.

STEP 20

Rubber cement the flesh side of the top edge of the lining collars. Fold the top edge of the lining collars over ³/₈" (1 cm).

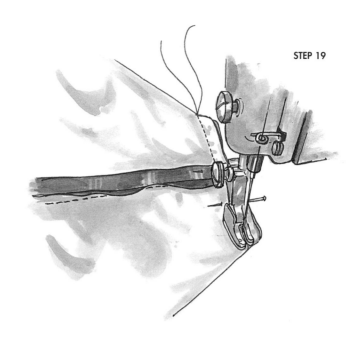

STEP 19

STEP 21

Drop the lining into the assembled outside with wrong sides together. *Keep in mind that the pocket goes in the back of the bag.*

STEP 22

Rubber cement around the top edge of the lining and the outside. Adhere the lining to the outside. Topstitch around the top edge of the bag ⅛" (3 mm) from the edge using a gauge foot or Teflon foot.

STEP 23

Topstitch around the handles ⅛" (3 mm) from the edge using a gauge foot. Punch the holes for the rivets using a #2 punch.

STEP 24

Punch the four holes for the grommets through the outside and lining using ½" (1.3 cm) punch. *Punch one hole at a time using the punching board inside the bag.*

STEP 25

Set the grommets using a grommet-setting kit.

STEP 26

Pull the handles through the grommets, and set the rivets in the holes using a rivet-setting kit.

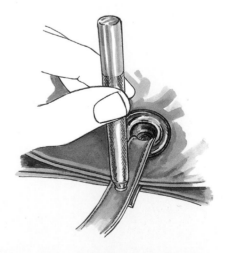

envelope bag

Funky and festive, this envelope bag is perfect for any occasion. Sporting a short top handle, our bag is right on the fashion mark. Dressed up with snakeskin appliqués in contrasting colors or, alternatively, toned down with muted leathers, your envelope bag is sure to strike the right cord.

MATERIALS

- 2¾ square feet (0.3 sq. m) of 2 to 3 oz. leather for outside
- 2¾ (0.2 sq. m) square feet of 1½ to 2 oz. leather for lining
- 120 square inches (774 sq. cm) of snakeskin (or other thin contrasting leather)
- 4 yards (3.5 m) of thin leather cording
- Six ⁵⁄₁₆" (8 mm) long rivets
- 2 D-rings ¾" (1.9 cm) wide
- 1 O-ring ¾" (1.9 cm) wide
- 1 collar button
- Rubber cement
- Double-sided craft tape (¼" [5 mm] wide)
- 14" × 18" (36 cm × 46 cm) sheet of craft foam
- 15" × 8" (38 cm × 20 cm) piece of heavyweight fusible interfacing
- Acrylic leather paint or edge dye

TOOLS

- Contrasting thread
- Rotary or handheld leather hole punches, sizes #2 and #6
- Rivet-setting kit
- Rawhide mallet or hammer
- Bone folder
- Silver pen for marking leather
- Awl
- Large metal ruler
- Scissors
- Utility or craft knife
- Cutting mat
- Masking tape and/or pattern weights
- Binder clips
- Cotton swabs, wool dauber, or small paintbrush

MACHINERY

Home sewing machine with leather needle, gauge foot, and Teflon foot

GETTING STARTED

Enlarge and cut out all envelope bag patterns, following the instructions on the patterns. All pieces should be cut out separately except for the handle, tabs for handle, front tab, and back/flap tab, which have special instructions.

When cutting leather or materials for patterns, either loop masking tape onto the back of the patterns or use pattern weights to keep patterns in place while cutting. *Note: Always test leather before using masking tape to hold down your pattern. Masking tape may remove the finish from the leather or leave a mark on it.*

Line up the metal ruler along the straight edges of the patterns, and cut the leather with the utility or craft knife. Let the edge of the ruler guide the knife as you cut. When cutting rounded edges, simply use the edge of your pattern as a guide. *Note: Be sure to cut on a proper surface.*

Transfer the hole markings and appliqué and tab placements to the outside front and outside pieces by pinning through with the awl, or marking with a silver pen through holes punched into the patterns.

SPECIAL CUTTING INSTRUCTIONS

For Handle

Cut out one piece of snakeskin and one piece of outside leather, each measuring 10½" × 1" (27 cm × 2.5 cm). Rubber cement the flesh sides together. Then cut from the handle pattern. Mark and then punch size #2 holes for the rivet placement.

For Front Tab

Cut out two pieces of snakeskin and one piece of outside leather, each measuring 1" × 4½" (2.5 cm × 11 cm). Rubber cement the layers together to create a "sandwich" with the good sides of the snakeskin facing out and the leather piece in the middle. Then cut from the front tab pattern. Mark for collar button placement. Punch a size #6 hole with a slit as noted on the pattern by using the hole punch, then slitting one end with a craft knife.

For Back/Flap Tab

Cut out one piece each of snakeskin and outside leather, each measuring 1" × 14" (2.5 cm × 35.6 cm). Rubber cement them together, flesh sides facing each other. Cut out from back/flap tab pattern. Mark for rivet placement.

After cutting out these pieces, apply acrylic paint or dye around their edges using a cotton swab, a wool dauber, or a paintbrush. Keep a damp cloth nearby to wipe off any excess. (We used yellow acrylic paint.)

STEP 1

Reinforce the front and back/flap by rubber cementing craft foam to the flesh side of the outside pieces. Reinforce the gussets and the bottom by ironing the fusible interfacing to the flesh side of the outside pieces.

STEP 2

Apply corner appliqués to the outside front and back pieces by adhering with double-sided craft tape or rubber cement. Topstitch all around, ⅛" (3 mm).

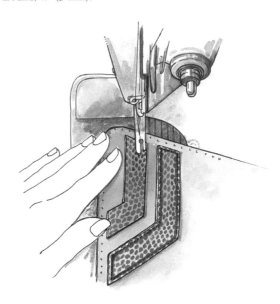

STEP 3

Wrap the back/flap tab around the O-ring, as noted on the pattern. Use double-sided craft tape to keep it in place. Place down on outside back/flap, using double-sided craft tape, and topstitch all around, close to the edge.

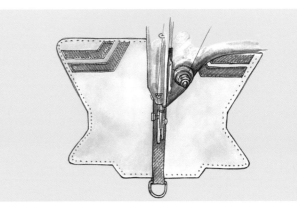

STEP 4

Topstitch around the edge of the front tab, as noted on the pattern. Then place the front tab on the outside front and topstitch around the remaining sides and bottom. Start and end the stitch by overlapping stitching on the sides by approximately ¼" (5 mm) (A). Punch a size #6 hole for the collar button through both the front tab and the outside front, as marked (B). Attach the collar button by screwing it together or setting it with a rawhide mallet (depending on the type of collar button used) (C).

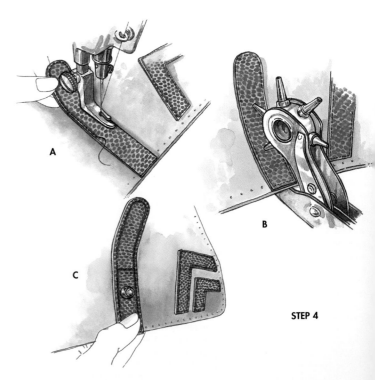

A

B

C

STEP 4

STEP 5

Topstitch the handle all around, ⅛" (3 mm) away from the edge with a gauge foot or Teflon foot. Then loop each end of the handle around the curved end of the D-ring. Attach on each side by setting rivets through the holes in handle. Loop a handle tab around each D-ring. Use double-sided craft tape to keep the ends pressed flat together. Topstitch all around each tab, ⅛" (3 mm) away from the edge of the "triangular" part of the tabs only. Be sure to match up the edges of both ends of the tab perfectly so that you are sewing through all the layers.

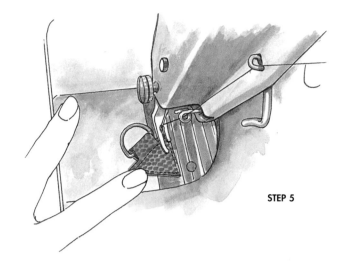

STEP 5

STEP 6

Stitch the outside gussets to the outside bottom, good sides facing each other, and matching up seam allowances (A). Repeat for the leather lining pieces. Rubber cement the inside seams for both and press them open with a bone folder (B). Hammer the seams flat. Attach the entire outside bottom/gusset section to the lining bottom/gusset section by rubber cementing the entire flesh side of both sections to each other. *Note: Be sure to match up the outer edges and seams perfectly.* Topstitch the top edges of the gussets, ⅛" (3 mm) close to the edge.

STEP 6

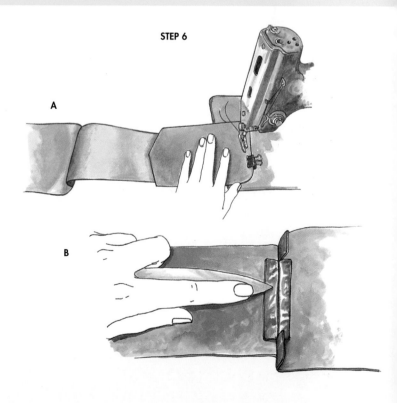

A

B

STEP 7

Carefully attach the outside front to the lining front by rubber cementing the flesh sides to each other. Topstitch across the top, staying ⅛" (3 mm) away from the edge.

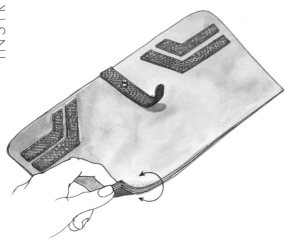

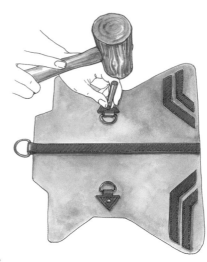

STEP 8

Carefully attach the outside back/flap to the lining back/flap by rubber cementing the flesh sides to each other. Place the handle tabs on the flap as noted on the pattern, punch size #2 holes through all the layers, and set with rivets. Also, punch a size #2 hole, and set a rivet through the back/flap tab, as marked.

STEP 9

Match up outer edges of front to outer edges of bottom gussets by using double-sided craft tape and binder clips to keep it in place. Be sure to pivot the corner of the gusset to match up with the bottom, as shown (A). Mark and then punch holes all around both layers at the same time, as marked on the front, using a leather hole punch (B). *Note: Be careful to keep the edges matched up together perfectly.*

STEP 9

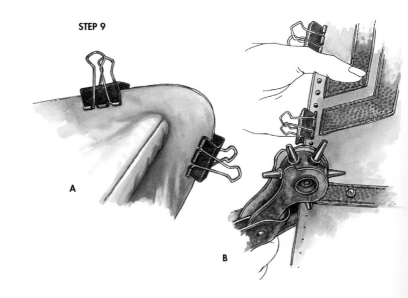

STEP 10

Stitch the front to the bottom/gussets by tying a knot at one end of the leather cording. Start lacing at the top inside corner of the gusset. Weave back and forth through the holes all around until you get to the inside top corner of the other gusset. Tie a secure knot and trim off excess cord. Repeat the same attachment process for the back/flap to the bottom/gussets by sticking them together, punching holes, and then lacing together. This time, tie a knot in the cord and start lacing from one of the center holes on the bottom. Weave all around the entire back/flap until you get to the last hole, next to the beginning hole. Tie a secure knot in the cord and cut off.

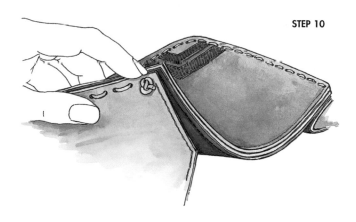

STEP 10

Styling Tip > Experiment with different edge-lacing techniques and your own customized appliqué shapes to create a more personalized look.

STEP 11

Apply acrylic paint or dye around all the edges of the bag using a cotton swab, wool dauber, or a thin paintbrush. Keep a damp cloth nearby to wipe off any excess.

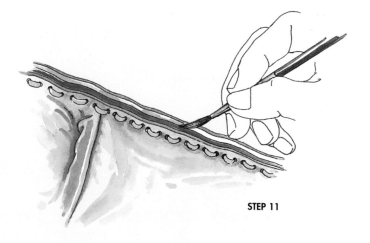

STEP 11

duffel bag

Handbag styles come and go but the duffel bag has remained a fashion statement for decades. The original duffel was used by athletes to carry their exercise clothing and equipment to and from the gym. This bag was large and cumbersome, definitely not a fashion item. It wasn't until the 1950s that handbag designers began to notice the duffel bag shape as a possible fashion silhouette. With some tweaking and changes in size, the lowly duffel became an elegant and stylish double-handled bag that women could wear for any occasion. Whether it remained large and softly constructed or small and somewhat rigid, the duffel bag had arrived on the fashion front with attitude.

Our "purple passion" duffel bag is no exception. With its snakeskin shoulder-length handles woven through the body to its neon yellow piping, this bag is both sporty and fashion right. Perfect for a day in the city or a night on the town.

MATERIALS

- 5 square feet (0.5 sq. m) of 2 to 3 oz. leather for outside
- 125 square inches (806 sq. cm) of snakeskin (or other thin contrasting leather)
- 36" (91.5 cm) of premade piping (or 1" × 36" [2.5 cm × 91.5 cm] of contrasting leather and 36" [91.5 cm] of ¹/₈" [3 mm] thick cording)
- ¼ yard (23 cm) of lining fabric
- Two ⁵/₁₆" (8 mm) long rivets
- Six ³/₁₆" (4.7 mm) eyelets
- Two ¾" (1.9 cm) buckles
- 12" (30.5 cm) zipper
- Matching and contrasting thread for machine sewing

TOOLS

- Rotary or handheld leather hole punches, sizes #2 and #6
- ¾" (1.9 cm) oblong punch
- Rivet-setting kit
- Eyelet-setting kit
- Utility or craft knife
- Awl
- Bone folder
- 12" (30.5 cm) and 36" (91.5 cm) metal rulers
- Masking tape and/or pattern weights
- Binder clips
- Scissors
- Straight pins for pinning lining material
- Rawhide mallet or hammer
- Fabric-marking pencil
- Cardboard, 8 oz. leather or wood for punching board

MACHINERY

Home sewing machine with leather, needle, gauge foot, zipper foot, and Teflon foot

GETTING STARTED

Cut out all leather and fabric pieces from the duffel bag patterns. All leather pieces should be cut separately. When cutting leather or materials for patterns, either loop masking tape onto the back of the patterns or use pattern weights to keep patterns in place while cutting.
Note: Always test leather before using masking tape to hold down your pattern. Masking tape may remove the finish from the leather or leave a mark on it.

Line up the metal ruler along the straight edges of the patterns and cut the leather with the utility or craft knife. When cutting rounded edges, simply use the edge of the pattern as a guide. *Note: Be sure to cut on a proper surface.*

Use a fabric-marking pencil to trace patterns onto the lining fabric, and cut out the pieces with scissors.

SPECIAL CUTTING INSTRUCTIONS

Cut out two pieces of snakeskin and two pieces of outside leather, each measuring 1" × 30" (2.5 cm × 76 cm). Rubber cement each snakeskin piece to an outside leather piece with the flesh sides together to create two 1" × 30" (2.5 cm × 76 cm) strips. Use the handle pattern to cut the pieces to the correct width. Transfer the hole placements for the eyelets.

Repeat the same steps for the buckle pieces, cutting the strips 1" × 9" (2.5 cm × 23 cm), cement them together and cut them to size using the pattern. Transfer the hole placements for the buckle and rivets.

Making Piping (See illustrations below)
Rubber cement the cording in the center of the 1" × 36" (2.5 cm × 91.5 cm) piece of contrasting leather (A). Fold the leather over the cording, matching up the raw edges of the leather. Use a bone folder to sandwich the cording into place (B). Use scissors to clip every ¹/₈" (3 mm) along the seam allowance of the piping (C). *Note: Do not clip all the way to cording, or it will show in the finished duffel bag.*

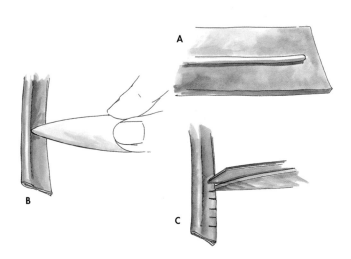

STEP 1

Punch slots with ¾" (1.9 cm) oblong punch through the outside front and back leather pieces. Always use a piece of cardboard, heavy leather, or wood under the leather when using a drive punch.

STEP 2

Cut a 1" × 1" (2.5 cm × 2.5 cm) tab to cover the ends of the piping. Begin sewing the piping to the outside leather gussets, centering the piping on top of the tab. Use a zipper foot to sew the piping all around the gusset with the raw edges lined up (A). Cut the piping so that it butts up to the beginning piece. Fold the tab over the piping ends, and stitch the tab down (B).

STEP 3

Repeat Step 2 for the other gusset.

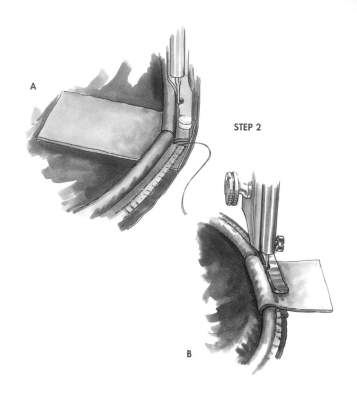

STEP 2

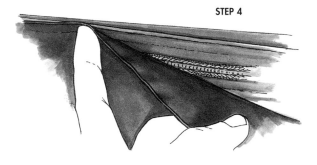

STEP 4

STEP 4

Sew the zipper between the outside leather and lining using ⅜" (1 cm) seam allowance, back tacking at the beginning and end of the stitch line. Be sure the right side of the zipper is facing the right side of the leather.

STEP 5

Repeat Step 4 for the other side of the zipper.

STEP 6

Topstitch the seam on either side of the zipper ⅛" (3 mm) away from the edge using a gauge foot.

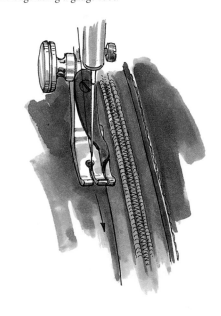

STEP 7

Topstitch all around the handles and buckle straps ⅛" (0.3 cm) away from the edge with a gauge foot. Punch all holes in handles and buckle straps, as labeled on the patterns.

STEP 8

Set eyelets with the eyelet-setting kit.

STEP 9

Place buckles on the straps, and set the rivets with the rivet-setting kit.

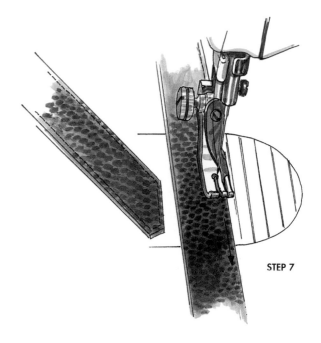

STEP 7

STEP 10

Weave handles and buckle straps through the front and back outside leather pieces.

STEP 11

Stitch the ends of the handles' and buckles' straps in place within the seam allowance along the bottom edge.

STEP 12

Rubber cement the bottom edge together, lining up the handles and buckle straps. Stitch the bottom edge together using ³/₈" (1 cm) seam allowance.

STEP 13

Rubber cement the bottom seam open. Gently hammer the seam to get a flat finished seam.

STEP 14

Pin and partially stitch the bottom edge of the lining together using ³/₈" (1 cm) seam allowance. Leave a 6" (15 cm) opening in the bottom seam of the lining to turn the bag right side out in Step 18.

STEP 15

Clip the outside leather gusset to the outside front/back piece lining up the center bottom with the tab covering the piping joint (A). Pin and stitch the lining gussets to the lining front/back using ³/₈" (1 cm) seam allowance. Use the notches transferred from the pattern to match up the gusset and the front/back (B).

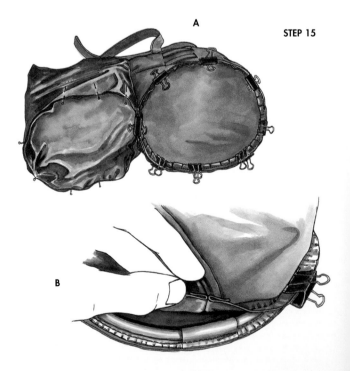

A

STEP 15

B

STEP 16

STEP 16

Sew with a zipper foot using the edge of the piping as a guide for the ³/₈" (1 cm) seam allowance. The lining will get sewn into the seam in the zipper area.

STEP 17

Repeat Steps 15 and 16 for the other side of the bag.

Styling Tip > Go crazy. Change the color of the zipper. Make the piping the same color. Or change the size of the buckles and handles. Make your duffel fit your personality.

STEP 18

Turn the duffel bag right side out through the opening in the bottom seam of the lining.

STEP 19

Fold and pin the bottom seam of the lining closed. Topstitch the lining closed.

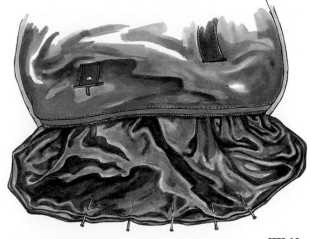

STEP 19

hobo bag

As the name states, this bag silhouette originated in the early 1900s when so-called hobos would tie their belongings to a stick using a piece of fabric for support while on the move from one place to another. Their belongings would stay intact as they boarded the rails in search of work or shelter. The name and shape has stuck since that time, giving the bag its popularity and instant design recognition. Our hobo is made of distressed leather with a top zipper and eyelet and lace detailing on the handle as well as the body. The only trait that remains from its origin is the name—everything else is sophisticated and classic!

MATERIALS
- 7 square feet (0.7 sq. m) of 2 to 3 oz. leather for outside
- ¼ yard (23 cm) for lining fabric
- ¼ yard (23 cm) medium-weight Pellon interfacing or craft felt
- 17" (43 cm) zipper
- Ninety-six ⅛" (3 mm) eyelets
- Ten ¼" (5 mm) long rivets
- Two O-rings 1" (2.5 cm) wide
- Matching and contrasting thread for machine sewing
- Rubber cement

TOOLS
- Rotary or handheld leather hole punch, size #2
- Eyelet-setting kit
- Rivet-setting kit
- Utility or craft knife
- Awl
- 24" (61 cm) metal ruler
- Masking tape and/or pattern weights
- Scissors
- Straight pins for pinning lining material
- Binder clips
- Fabric-marking pencil
- Rawhide mallet or hammer
- Cardboard, 8 oz. leather, or wood for punching board

MACHINERY
Home sewing machine with leather needle, ⅛" (3 mm) gauge foot, and Teflon foot

GETTING STARTED
Cut out all leather and fabric pieces from the hobo bag patterns. All the leather pieces should be cut separately.

When cutting leather or materials for patterns, either loop masking tape onto the back of the patterns or use pattern weights to keep patterns in place while cutting. *Note: Always test leather before using masking tape to hold down your pattern. Masking tape may remove the finish from the leather or leave a mark on it.*

Line up the metal ruler along the straight edges of the pattern, and cut the leather with the utility or craft knife. When cutting rounded edges, simply use the edge of the pattern as a guide. *Note: Be sure to cut on a proper surface.*

Use a fabric-marking pencil to trace patterns onto the lining fabric and felt, and cut out the pieces with scissors Transfer the hole placements for the rivets and the eyelets.

STEP 1

Rubber cement around the edges on the flesh side of the center and side panel pieces and around the Pellon. Adhere the Pellon to the flesh side of the leather ³⁄₈" (1 cm) below the top edge. If the Pellon extends beyond the leather edge, trim the Pellon.

STEP 2

Using the binder clips, attach front center panel to a front side panel along its corresponding ³⁄₈" (1 cm) seam allowance edge, good sides facing each other. Sew pieces together using a Teflon foot, back tacking at the beginning and end of the stitch line. Repeat with opposite front side panel to other half of front center panel.

STEP 2

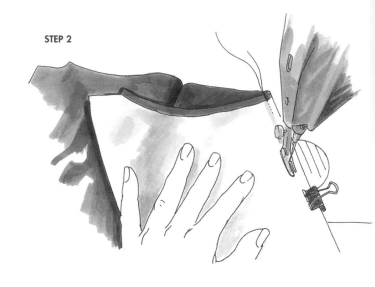

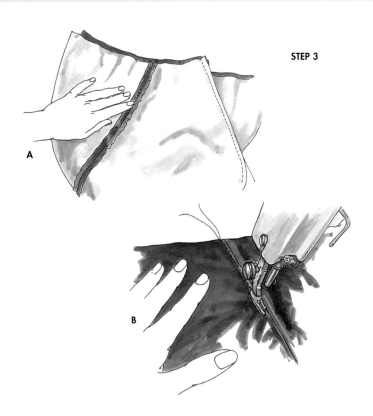

STEP 3

STEP 3

Using rubber cement, glue and press the seam allowances open; hammer them flat (A). Topstitch at ¹⁄₈" (3 mm) on either side of each seam using the gauge or Teflon foot (B).

STEP 4

Repeat Steps 2 and 3 for the back half of the bag.

STEP 5

Punch holes through leather and Pellon front and back pieces, as labeled on patterns. Set eyelets with the eyelet-setting kit.

STEP 6

Cut four 45" (114.5 cm) long pieces from the lacing. Lace each piece through eyelets using a crisscross stitch across each seam. Start with equal lengths of each end of lacing coming through top two holes; crisscross in and out of holes until both ends come through back side of last two holes. Tie ends together securely inside bag. Trim off any excess.

STEP 6

STEP 7

Clip and sew the zipper between the outside leather and lining using ⅜" (1 cm) seam allowance, back tacking at the beginning and end of the stitch line Be sure the right side of the zipper is facing the right side of the leather.

STEP 8

Repeat Step 7 for the other side of the zipper.

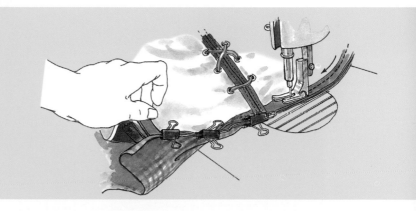

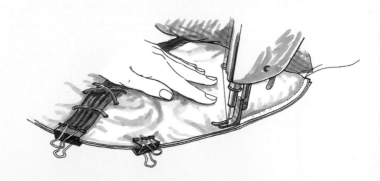

STEP 10

Clip all around the sides and bottom of the outside front and back pieces together, good sides facing each other. Using the Teflon foot, stitch all around the sides and bottom on the ⅜" (3 mm) seam allowance line, back tacking at the beginning and the end of the stitch line. Be sure to unzip the zipper before sewing! There will be a small opening on either side of zipper on outside leather and lining; this will be closed in Step 23 when tabs are riveted to bag.

STEP 9

Topstitch the seam on either side of the zipper ⅛" (3 mm) away from the edge using a gauge foot.

STEP 11

Using the Teflon foot, stitch all four "darts" on the corner lining pieces at ⅜" (3 mm) seam allowance, good sides facing together.

STEP 12

Pin and partially stitch the lining together at ⅜" (1 cm) seam allowance, leaving a 6" (15 cm) wide opening in the center bottom to turn the bag right side out.

STEP 13

Turn the bag right side out through the opening in the bottom seam of the lining.

STEP 12

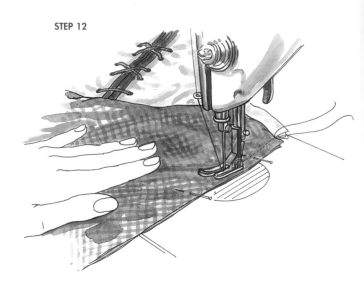

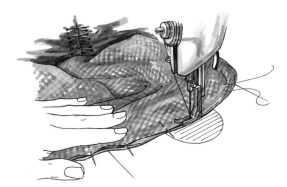

STEP 14

Fold, pin, and topstitch the opening of the lining closed.

STEP 15

Pinch the opened top corners of bag flat, and punch holes for rivets, as noted on patterns; these will be for attaching tabs to bag. Be sure to keep zipper centered.

STEP 16

Rubber cement the flesh side of the leather handle. To create a "trifold" handle, adhere one-third of the handle down by folding as marked on pattern. Rubber cement the surface of the folded third, then adhere the flesh side of the other side on top of it, being sure edge of leather is neatly lined up along the folded edge of the handle. Lightly hammer handle flat.

STEP 17

Topstitch all around handle using the ⅛" (3 mm) gauge foot.

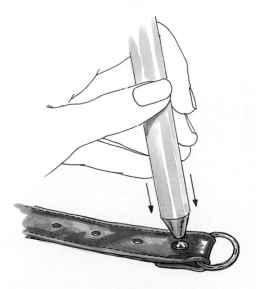

STEP 18

Punch holes through leather handle, as labeled on patterns. Set eyelets with the eyelet-setting kit. Wrap ends of handle around O-rings, and set rivets with the rivet-setting kit.

STEP 19

Lace remaining lacing through the eyelets of the handle. Start by making a secure knot at the end of lacing, and come up through a hole at one end of handle, with knot on the inside. Loop lace around handle, and go back through same hole from topside toward the inside. Then lace down the handle, through each eyelet, alternating back and forth from one side of handle to the other. End off lacing in similar fashion to how it was started off, being sure to tie a secure knot in the end.

STEP 20

Rubber cement and adhere flesh side of both tab linings to the flesh side of outside tabs. Rubber cement the exposed flesh edges of outside tabs over edges of lining tabs all around. Fold down using bone folder and lightly hammer flat.

STEP 21

Topstitch all around tabs using the gauge foot.

STEP 22

Punch holes through tabs as marked on patterns.

STEP 23

Fold tabs through O-rings. Secure tabs closed around them by setting rivets through top two holes closest to O-rings (A). Insert top corners of bag between ends of tabs. Set rivets through remaining two holes of each tab through holes in top corners of bag, to attach handle to bag (B).

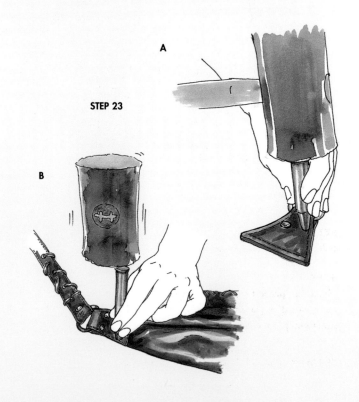

belt and belt bag

It's a belt, no, wait a minute—it's a bag. No, it's a belt bag! This clever creation was born out of the need to use our leisure time to its fullest. If you're biking, hiking, or window shopping, using a belt bag is the easiest way to carry your personal items with you, without having to worry about the excess weight on your shoulder or hand. The belt holds the bag securely to your waist, making this accessory perfect for sport activities or for tooling around on a relaxing weekend. The bag can also be removed, giving you the option of wearing the belt alone.

Our belt bag ensemble features two-tone leather with racing stripe accent on the belt, along with a coordinated two-tone leather high-tech asymmetric pocketed bag sure to stop everyone in his or her tracks. This bag is a fashion must for every athletically minded "fashionista."

For Belt

MATERIALS
- 2½" × 44" (6.5 cm × 112 cm) of 2 to 3 oz. leather for outside
- 2½" × 44" (6.5 cm × 112 cm) of 1½ to 2 oz. leather for lining
- 1" × 44" (2.5 cm × 112 cm) of leather for the trim (stripe)
- Sixteen ⅜" (1 cm) grommets
- Four ⁵⁄₁₆" (8 mm) long rivets
- One 1⅜" (3.5 cm) buckle
- Matching and contrasting thread for machine sewing
- Rubber cement
- Double-sided craft tape (¼" [0.5 cm] wide)

TOOLS
- Rotary or handheld leather hole punch, size ⁵⁄₁₆" (8 mm)
- Oblong punch to fit around the buckle
- Rivet-setting kit
- Grommet-setting kit
- Utility or craft knife
- Awl
- 48" (122 cm) metal rulers
- Masking tape and/or pattern weights
- Scissors
- Stapler
- Rawhide mallet or hammer
- Cardboard, 8 oz. leather, or wood for punching board
- #1 Handheld punch

MACHINERY
Home sewing machine with leather needle, ⅛" (3 mm) gauge foot, ¹⁄₁₆" (1.6 mm) gauge foot, and Teflon foot

GETTING STARTED
Cut out belt as described in Special Cutting Instructions.

When cutting leather or materials for patterns, either loop masking tape onto the back of the patterns or use pattern weights to keep patterns in place while cutting. *Note: Always test leather before using masking tape to hold down your pattern. Masking tape may remove the finish from the leather or leave a mark on it.*

Line up the metal ruler along the straight edges of the patterns, and cut the leather with the utility or craft knife. *Note: Be sure to cut on a proper surface.*

SPECIAL CUTTING INSTRUCTIONS
Rubber cement the two pieces of 2½" × 44" (6.5 cm × 112 cm) pieces together, flesh sides facing each other. Cut out using belt pattern. Also cut belt keeper from pattern.

STEP 1

Cut out center stripe from pattern. Using double-sided craft tape, place on outside of belt as marked on pattern.

STEP 2

Sew the long ends of the stripe to the belt using a $\frac{1}{16}$" (1.6 mm) gauge foot.

STEP 2

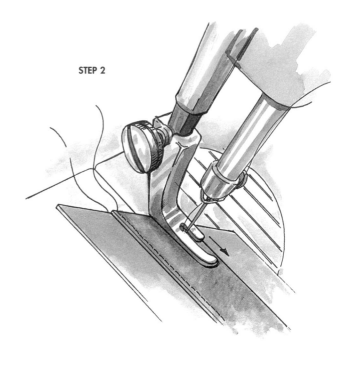

STEP 3

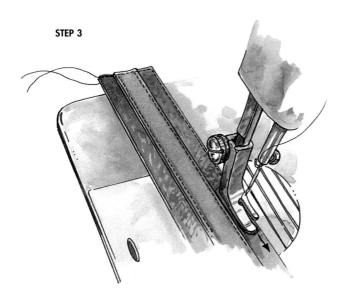

STEP 3

Sew all around the edge of the keeper using the $\frac{1}{16}$" (1.6 mm) gauge foot.

STEP 4

Sew all around the outer edge of the belt using the $\frac{1}{8}$" (3 mm) gauge.

STEP 5

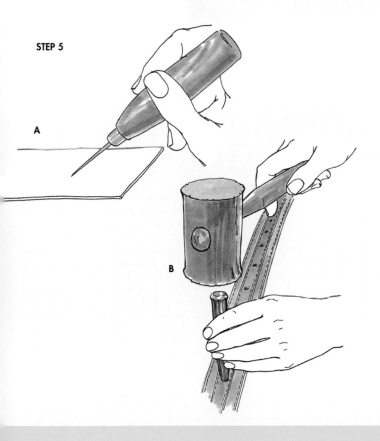

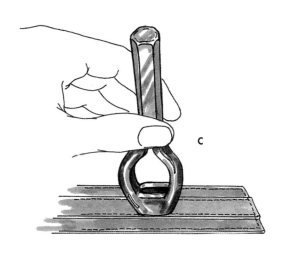

STEP 5

Transfer grommet, rivet and oblong hole placement onto belt using an awl (A). Punch holes using #1 hole punch and rawhide mallet or hammer (B). Also punch out oblong hole with punch as marked on pattern (C).

STEP 6

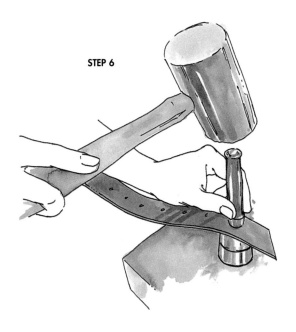

STEP 6

Set grommets on belt with grommet-setting kit.

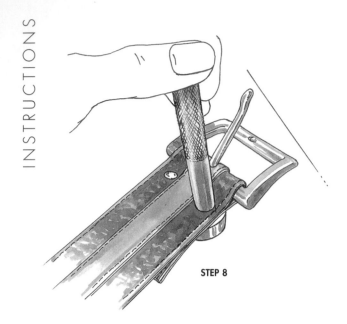

STEP 8

STEP 7
Wrap belt around buckle, placing prong of buckle through oblong hole.

STEP 8
Punch holes for rivets, and set the first two closest to the buckle using a rivet-setting kit.

STEP 9
Using a stapler, staple the ends of the belt keeper so they are butted together. If staples do not hold, hand stitch them together.

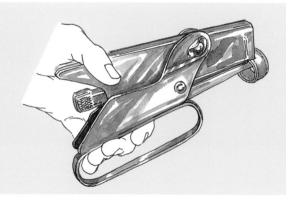

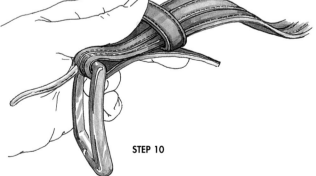

STEP 10

STEP 10
Slip the keeper onto the belt so the stapled ends are sandwiched between the two layers of the folded belt.

STEP 11
Punch holes and set the last two rivets, making sure to enclose the belt loop between the belt layers.

for the bag

Cut out belt loops as described in Special Cutting Instructions. When cutting leather or materials for patterns, either loop masking tape onto the back of the patterns or use pattern weights to keep patterns in place while cutting. Transfer window cutouts for zipper onto outside front and pocket pieces by using an awl. Remove pattern and cut window out with a knife (See below). *Note: Always test leather before using masking tape to hold down your pattern. Masking tape may remove the finish from the leather or leave a mark on it.*

Line up the metal ruler along the straight edges of the patterns, and cut the leather with the utility or craft knife. *Note: Be sure to cut on a proper surface.*

SPECIAL CUTTING INSTRUCTIONS

Rubber cement two 10" × 1½" (25.5 cm × 4 cm) pieces of leather together, flesh sides facing each other. These will be for the belt attachment loops. Cut from strap #1 and strap #2 patterns. Transfer hole placements onto straps using an awl.

MATERIALS
- 1⅓ square feet (0.1 sq. m) of 2 to 3 oz. leather for outside
- 6" (15 cm) of 1½ to 2 oz. contrasting leather for pocket and belt loops
- Two 7" (18 cm) zippers
- 2 collar buttons
- Matching and contrasting thread for machine sewing
- Rubber cement
- Double-sided craft tape (¼" wide) (5 mm)

TOOLS
- Rotary or handheld leather hole punches, sizes #2 and #6
- Utility or craft knife
- Awl
- 12" (30.5 cm) metal ruler
- Scissors
- Masking tape and/or pattern weights
- Rawhide mallet or hammer
- Cardboard, 8 oz. leather, or wood for punching board

MACHINERY
Home sewing machine with leather needle, ⅛" (3 mm) gauge foot, 1/16" (1.6 mm) gauge foot

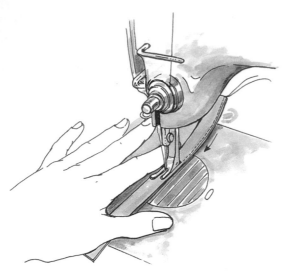

STEP 1
Topstitch all around the straps using a ¹/₁₆" (1.6 mm) gauge foot.

STEP 2
Punch a size #2 hole for the collar pin attachment using a hole punch. Attach collar buttons to straps (by either screwing in or setting, depending on type purchased) (A). Punch a size #6 hole with a slit, as marked on pattern, for the collar button to go through (B).

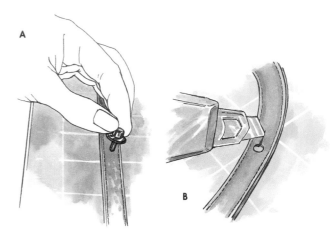

STEP 3
Adhere the double-sided craft tape to the flesh sides of the front and pocket pieces, all around the window openings.

STEP 4
Place zippers so they are centered in the cutouts. For the front piece, have the zipper run from left to right; for the pocket zipper, have the zipper run from right to left. Trim off any excess from the zippers.

STEP 5
Topstitch zippers all around openings using the ¹/₈" (3 mm) gauge foot.

STEP 5

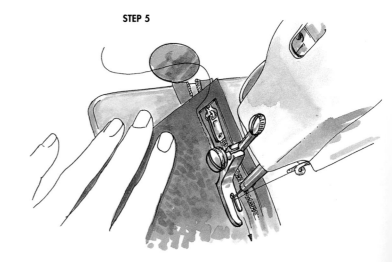

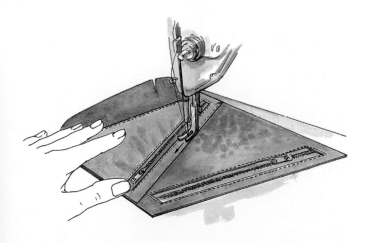

STEP 6

Adhere the double-sided craft tape to the flesh side of the pocket, all around the edges. Place onto front piece, as noted on pattern. Topstitch all around edge of pocket to front piece using the 1/8" (3 mm) gauge foot.

Adhere the double-sided craft tape to the flesh side of the front piece along the inner edges of the two darts. Overlap and stick the corner so the inner half of dart meets up with the notch. Topstitch corners in place using the 1/8" (3 mm) gauge foot. Trim away excess bulk from the flesh side with scissors.

STEP 8

Adhere the double-sided craft tape to the flesh side of outside back piece, all around the edges. Place straps 1 and 2 in place, as noted on patterns. Stick onto front piece, sandwiching straps in between. Be careful to perfectly match up the edges all around. Use binder clips to hold the corners in place. Topstitch all around edge of front piece using the 1/8" (3 mm) gauge foot.

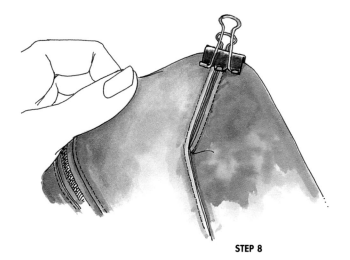

STEP 8

cell phone holder

Who would have thought that just a few years ago people got along without cell phones? That must have been in the previous century, right? But, here we are with a cell phone attached to our clothing, carried in our purse, or tucked discretely into a briefcase or tote. We have become connected to friends, family, and work. However, even though we must remain tethered to this new device, it doesn't mean we have to sacrifice style. Our cell phone holder hits the fashion target head on with its lizard arrow and streamlined shape. Use the cell phone holder by itself, or coordinate it with a Belt and Belt Bag (page 51) for a perfect ensemble.

MATERIALS

- ¾ square feet (0.2 m) of 2 to 3 oz. leather for outside
- 77 square inches (497 sq. cm) of lizard (or other thin contrasting leather) for appliqué and belt loop
- One ½" × ¾" (1 cm × 2 cm) of hook-and-loop fastener
- Matching and contrasting thread for machine sewing
- Rubber cement
- Double-sided craft tape (¼" [5 mm] wide)

TOOLS

- Utility or craft knife
- Awl
- 12" (30.5 cm) metal ruler
- Masking tape and/or pattern weights
- Scissors
- Cardboard, 8 oz. leather, or wood for punching board

MACHINERY

Home sewing machine with leather needle, ¹⁄₁₆" (1.6 mm) gauge foot, ⅛" (3 mm) gauge foot, Teflon foot

GETTING STARTED

Cut out belt loop as described in Special Cutting Instructions. When cutting leather or materials for patterns, either loop masking tape onto the back of the patterns or use pattern weights to keep patterns in place while cutting. *Note: Always test leather before using masking tape to hold down your pattern. Masking tape may remove the finish from the leather or leave a mark on it.*

Line up the metal ruler along the straight edges of the patterns, and cut the leather with the utility or craft knife. *Note: Be sure to cut on a proper surface.*

SPECIAL CUTTING INSTRUCTIONS

Rubber cement one piece of lizard and one piece of outside leather together, each measuring 1" × 3" (2.5 cm × 7.5 cm) as shown below. Keep flesh sides facing each other. Cut out using belt loop pattern.

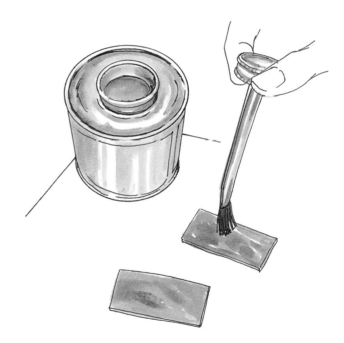

STEP 1

Topstitch down the sides of outer edge of belt loop using
1/16" (1.6 mm) gauge foot.

STEP 2

Trim hook-and-loop fastener into a point shape, as on flap pattern. Stick the loop part to the flap of the leather lining as noted on pattern, using the double-sided craft tape (A). Stitch in place using 1/8" (3 mm) gauge foot (B).

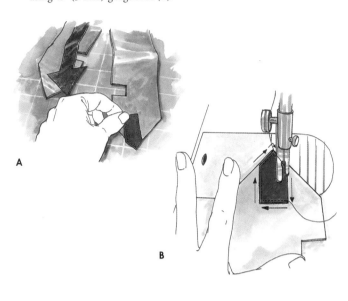

STEP 3

Place lizard appliqué down center of outside front piece, as noted on pattern. Topstitch all around using the 1/16" (1.6 mm) gauge foot.

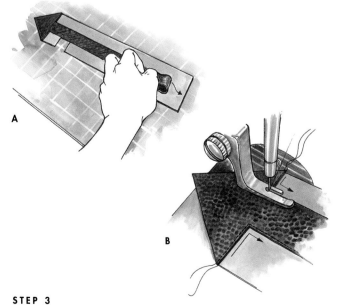

STEP 4

Stick hook part of fastener to the front, on top of trim, as noted on pattern, using the double-sided craft tape. Topstitch all around using the 1/8" (3 mm) gauge foot.

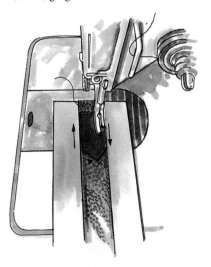

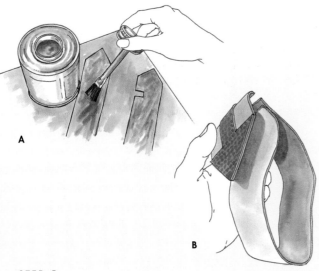

A

B

STEP 6

Place belt loop down on back of cell phone holder, as noted on pattern. Stitch securely across the top and bottom of strip only using the Teflon foot.

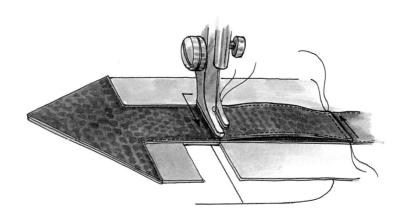

STEP 5

Rubber cement the entire flesh sides of the outside and lining pieces (A). Stick them together, being careful to match up outer edges all around. Try to keep a "curve" in the flap and bottom part, to help it conform to phone shape (B).

Styling Tip >

Think big and bigger yet. Lengthen the pattern to fit larger cell phones. Substitute exotic leathers. Make your cell phone holder multicolored or tone on tone. This holder is perfect for making a "high-tech" statement in any arena. And, don't forget the men in your life…they could use some sprucing up, don't you think?

STEP 7

Topstitch around entire outer edge of cell phone holder using the ⅛" (3 mm) gauge foot.

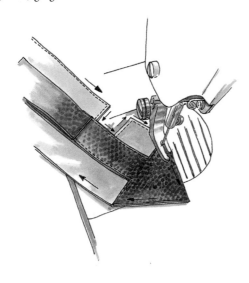

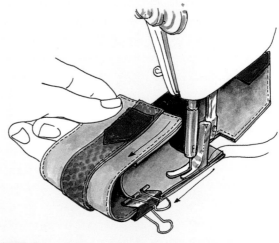

STEP 8

Adhere edges of gussets to inner edge of cell phone holder, as noted on pattern. Stitch in place using the ⅛" (3 mm) gauge foot. Start with the front of each half first, then attach the back half.

agenda book

Whether you use a book to keep your appointments organized or to keep a personal journal, our agenda book is the perfect fit. Just make sure that you fill it with the right style paper for each function. For example, if you are using the agenda for your appointments, find a calendar that shows a week at-a-glance or even a day at-a-glance. For your memoirs, use lined, quadrangle, or unlined paper.

Our agenda book features a personalized raised trapunto initial on the cover, along with inside pockets perfect for business cards, maps, or important papers. Use your imagination. Create a Grandmother's Brag Book by adding photo sheets, or use the book as a personal sketch pad by using unlined paper. Make the book special by using the initial to identify the function of each book (for example, use J for journal, S for sketches, or B for baby). You can even punch holes in envelopes and use the book as a coupon organizer.

MATERIALS
- 3 square feet (0.3 sq. m) of 1 to 2 oz. soft leather
- One 12" × 18' (30.5 cm × 5.5 m) piece of stiffened felt
- One 8½" × 11" (22 cm × 28 cm) piece of cardboard ¹⁄₁₆" (1.6 mm) thick
- One 3" × 3" (8 cm × 8 cm) piece of craft foam
- One 6" × 6" (15 cm × 15 cm) piece of stiff fusible interfacing
- 1 collar button
- Two ⁵⁄₁₆" (8 mm) long rivets
- Two ⁵⁄₈" (1.6 cm) long rivets
- 1 six-ring binder
- Heavy thread or embroidery thread for hand stitching
- Matching or contrasting thread for machine sewing

TOOLS
- Rotary or handheld leather hole punches, sizes #2 and #6
- Rivet-setting set
- Utility or craft knife
- Awl
- Metal ruler
- Scissors
- Masking tape and/or pattern weights
- Hammer
- Rawhide mallet or hammer
- Bone folder
- Rubber cement
- Cutting mat

MACHINERY
- Home sewing machine with leather needle, ¹⁄₈" (3 mm) gauge foot, and Teflon foot
- Iron

GETTING STARTED
Cut out all leather, felt, cardboard, and interfacing pieces as marked on the patterns. All the pieces should be cut separately.

When cutting leather or materials for patterns, either loop masking tape onto the back of the patterns or use pattern weights to keep patterns in place while cutting. *Note: Always test leather before using masking tape to hold down your pattern. Masking tape may remove the finish from the leather or leave a mark on it.*

Line up the metal ruler along the straight edges of the patterns, and cut the leather with a utility or craft knife. When cutting rounded edges, simply use the edge of your pattern as a guide. *Note: Be sure to cut on a proper surface.*

When cutting out the lining pockets, interfacing, and tab lining, be sure to flip the patterns. Cut knife lines in stiffened felt, making sure to stop at the breaks, to keep the felt in one piece.

STEP 1

Cut desired initial or motif out of the craft foam. When designing your motif, make sure it is not placed in the way of the collar button and tab.

STEP 2

Rubber cement the craft foam onto the stiffened felt.

STEP 3

Rubber cement the outside leather piece to the stiffened felt. Center the stiffened felt on the wrong side of the leather.

STEP 4

Use a bone folder to press the leather around the craft foam.

STEP 5

Use an awl to punch holes around the edge of the craft foam (A). Use heavy thread or embroidery thread to hand stitch around the craft foam. Stitch through the leather and the stiffened felt (B).

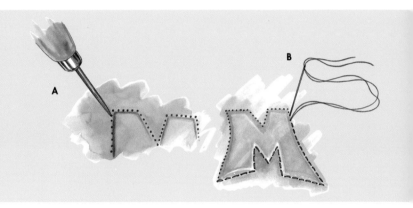

STEP 6

STEP 6

Rubber cement the cardboard reinforcements onto the back side of the stiffened felt. (See the pattern for their location.)

STEP 7

Rubber cement around the edge of the outside leather and the stiffened felt. Fold the leather over the edge of the stiffened felt using a bone folder.

STEP 8

Pleat the leather as it folds over the stiffened felt to create neat corners. Use scissors to cut out any bulk from the corners after the leather is folded over. Hammer the corners to flatten the pleats.

STEP 9

Use an awl to transfer the locations of the holes for the collar button and tab rivets. Punch size #2 holes using a leather hole punch.

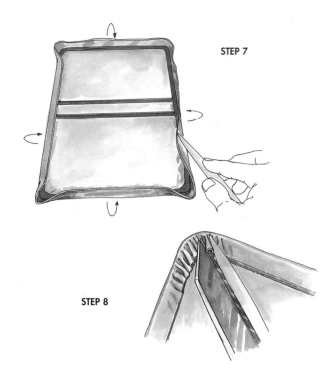

STEP 7

STEP 8

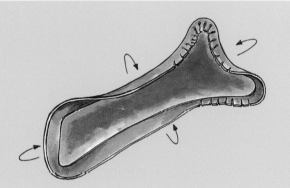

STEP 10

Rubber cement the stiffened felt to the outside leather for the tab. Rubber cement around the edge of the leather and the stiffened felt of the tab. Turn the edge of the leather over the stiffened felt. Make small cuts in the leather to the inside curve areas for a smooth turned edge. Pleat the leather around the corners, clip the excess away with scissors, and hammer the corners to flatten the pleats as in Step 7.

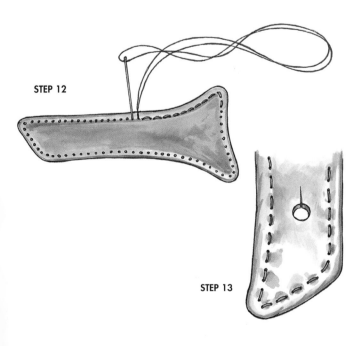

STEP 12

STEP 13

STEP 11

Rubber cement the raw-edge lining piece to the back side of the tab.

STEP 12

Use awl to punch holes around the tab ⅛" (3 mm) away from the edge. Use the same thread in Step 5 to hand stitch around the tab.

STEP 13

Transfer the location of the holes on the tab for the rivets and the collar button. Punch size #2 holes for the rivets using a leather hole punch. Punch a size #6 hole for the collar button. Cut a slit in the collar buttonhole, as illustrated, to create a "keyhole" for the collar button to fit into.

STEP 14

Screw or set collar button into place on the front portion of the outside.

STEP 15

Put the rivet post through the back portion of the outside into the tab. Press the rivet cap onto the post on the outside of the tab. Use a rawhide mallet and a rivet-setting kit to set the rivets.

STEP 16

Center the fusible interfacing on the lining pockets, and iron the fusible interfacing to the wrong sides of the lining pockets. *Note: Do not use steam.*

STEP 17

Transfer the card pocket placement onto the front pocket piece with an awl.

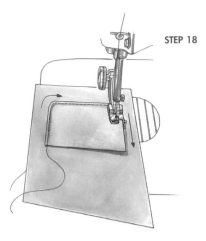

STEP 18

STEP 18

Rubber cement around the sides and bottom edges of the card pocket and around the placement location on the front lining pocket. Topstitch around the card pocket ⅛" (3 mm) away from the edge using a gauge foot or Teflon foot.

STEP 19

Rubber cement the lining pockets to the other two pieces cut out for the back of the lining pockets.

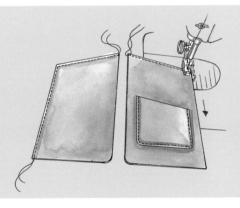

STEP 20

Topstitch across the top and inside edges of both pockets ⅛" (3 mm) away from the edge using a gauge foot or Teflon foot.

STEP 21

Transfer the lining pocket placements onto the lining piece with an awl.

STEP 22

Rubber cement around the bottom and outside edge of the lining pockets and around the placement locations on the lining piece.

STEP 23

Topstitch around the bottom and outside edge of the lining pockets ⅛" (3 mm) away from the edge using a gauge foot or Teflon foot.

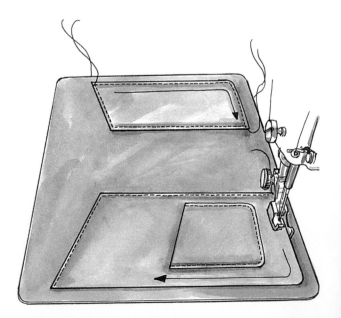

STEP 23

STEP 25

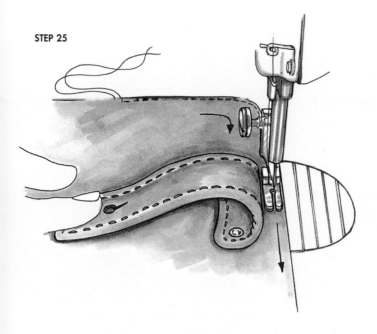

STEP 24

Rubber cement the lining to the wrong side of the outside piece.

STEP 25

Topstitch around the outside of the agenda ⅛" (0.3 cm) away from the edge using a gauge foot or Teflon foot. Be sure to lift the tab out of your way when you sew around the back portion.

STEP 26

Transfer the location of the rivet holes for the six-ring binder onto the outside with an awl. Punch size #2 holes through the agenda using a leather hole punch.

 *Styling Tip* >   Think color; use several different colored threads to give your book a "Technicolor" personality.

STEP 27

Line the six-ring binder up with the holes on the inside of the agenda. Put the rivet post through the binder and agenda. Press the rivet cap onto the post on the outside of the agenda. Set the rivet by putting an anvil under the cap (to preserve the dome of the cap) and use a setter over the hole of the rivet post. Hammer the setter with a rawhide mallet so that the binder is secure.

STEP 27

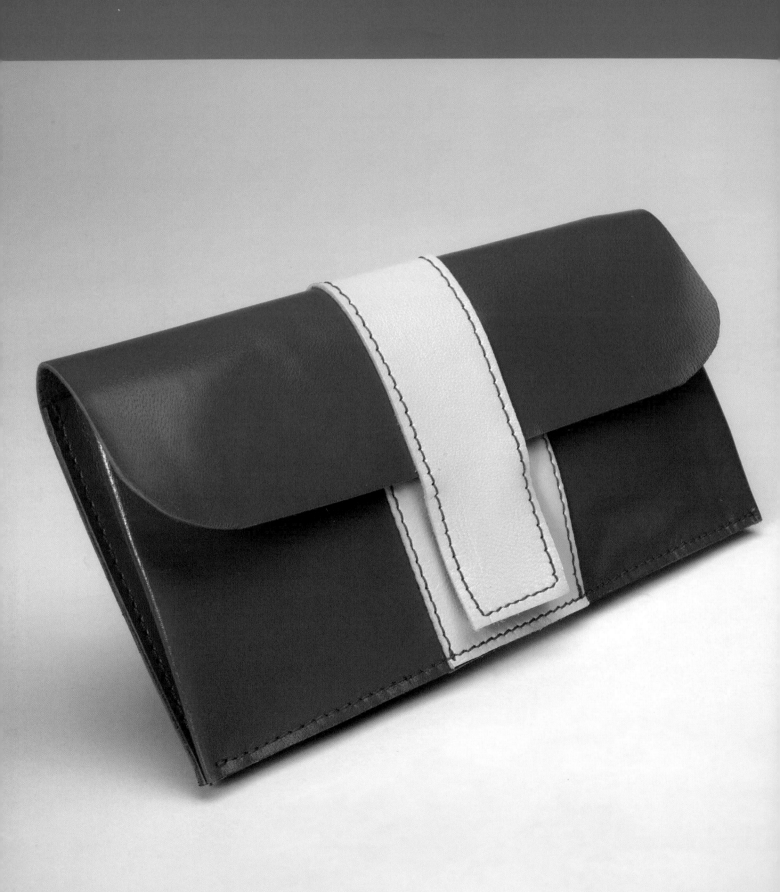

eyeglasses case

Eyeglasses have become one of the hottest fashion accessories. They come in a variety of shapes, sizes, and colors. Now you can create your own individualized eyeglasses case for that special eye-catching accessory. Use your imagination to create an eyeglasses case for every outfit in your closet. Or, better yet, make several for yourself and each of your friends and relatives.

MATERIALS

- 1 square foot (0.1 sq. m) of 2 to 3 oz. firm leather for outside
- 1 square foot (0.1 sq. m) of 2 to 3 oz. firm leather for appliqué
- 1" (2.5 cm) of hook-and-loop fastener
- Matching and contrasting thread for machine sewing
- Rubber cement

TOOLS

- Utility or craft knife
- Awl
- Metal ruler
- Masking tape and/or pattern weights
- Cutting board

MACHINERY

Home sewing machine with leather needle, ⅛" (3 mm) gauge foot, and Teflon foot

GETTING STARTED

Cut out all leather pieces and hook-and-loop fastener.

When cutting leather or materials for patterns, either loop masking tape onto the back of the patterns or use pattern weights to keep patterns in place while cutting. *Note: Always test leather before using tape to hold down your patterns. Tape may remove the finish from the leather or leave a mark.*

Line up the metal ruler along the straight edges of the patterns, and cut the leather with the utility or craft knife. When cutting rounded edges, simply use the edge of your pattern as a guide. *Note: Be sure to cut on a proper surface.*

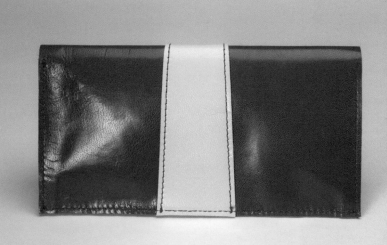

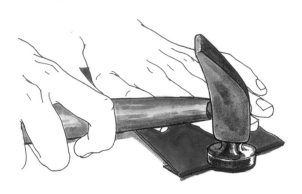

STEP 2

Use an awl to transfer the location of the hook-and-loop fastener on the appliqué pieces.

STEP 3

Use an awl to transfer the placement of the appliqué pieces onto the front and back.

STEP 1

Fold and hammer the front piece on lines noted on the pattern, to create two creases.

STEP 4

Rubber cement and stitch around 1 square inch (6.5 sq. cm) of hook-and-loop fastener onto the front appliqué piece.

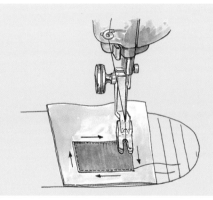

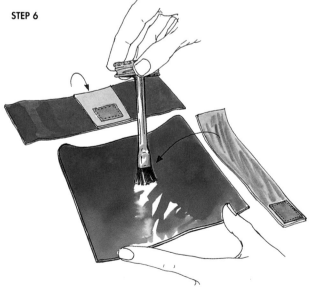

STEP 6

STEP 5

Rubber cement 1 square inch (6.5 sq. cm) of hook-and-loop fastener onto the wrong side of the back appliqué piece, as noted on the pattern.

STEP 6

Rubber cement the front and back appliqué pieces onto the front and back pieces.

STEP 7

Topstitch the appliqué pieces onto the front and back pieces along the side and top edges ⅛" (3 mm) away from the edge using a gauge foot or Teflon foot. Do not stitch across the bottom edges yet.

STEP 8

Rubber cement the side and bottom edges of the front and back pieces. Only cement the side edges of the back piece where the front meets it. Stick the two sides of the front and back together first, center the bottom edge by lining up the appliqué pieces, and then fold the front piece on the crease lines.

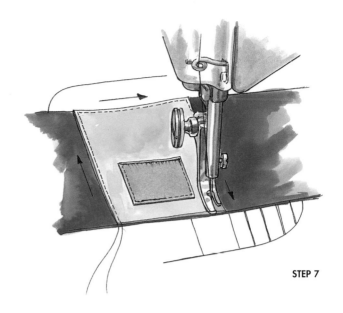

STEP 7

Styling Tip > Use contrasting leathers and threads to coordinate your eyeglasses case to your other personal accessories and handbags.

STEP 9

Topstitch down the side edges ⅛" (3 mm) away from the edge using a gauge foot or Teflon foot. Move the folded sections out of the way as you sew down the sides. Back tack at the top and bottom of the stitch line.

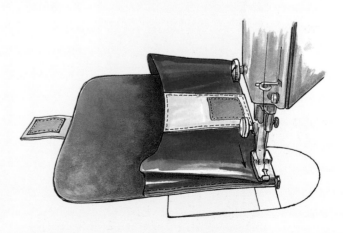

STEP 10

Topstitch across the bottom edge ⅛" (3 mm) away from the edge using a gauge foot or Teflon foot. Stitch over the folds to create side gussets and back tack at the beginning and end of the stitch line.

SECTION THREE

gallery

When it comes to accessories, Fashion Institute of Technology (FIT) is probably the most creative school in the United States. But then again, we're prejudiced! When we took on the assignment of creating this book, it was with the idea of giving the patterns to our students to see what they would do with the designs. Their assignment was to take the patterns and change them, modify them, and be as creative as they wanted. The following pages are the results of their creativity. Some students took the original pattern and modified only the flap or length of the handle or changed the material, whereas others went all out! Whatever they did, they brought our patterns and designs to a whole new level. They created new and exciting designs that are both fashion forward and trendy.

So, now it's your turn. Use their creations and ours as inspiration. Let your mind wander. Check out your drawers and closets for old knitted sweaters, pieces of jewelry, or old handbags that you can rip apart. Salvage only those parts that inspire you. Experiment with paint, dyes, and sewing techniques that you would use on garments. Bring your creative personality to every accessory you make.

Remember: You are only as good and as creative as you want to be. Take note of our accessories design students for they inspire great things from themselves and now from you!

Special thanks to the students from the BFA in Accessories Design and Fabrication for their interpretations of our patterns and for taking those designs over the top!

TITLE: LAX to JFK
STUDENT: Shelley Parker
PATTERNS: Duffel Bag, Cell Phone Holder, and Agenda Book

What better way to travel than with a coordinated collection of accessories featuring shocking pink zippers, contrasting detailed pink stitching, and, of course, the reflective gray "runway" signature stripe. The agenda book has an added pocket on the outside with contrasting zipper and stitch detailing, whereas the duffel sports shocking pink buckles and an extra zipper pocket on either side as well as across the top. This collection is both hot and sophisticated, sure to turn heads on both coasts.

TITLE: Charlotte's Web
STUDENT: Hannah Polgar
PATTERN: Envelope Bag

Charlotte would love to spin this fashionable web envelope bag. Made of burgundy suede, this bag features a double gold-metal, circular handle attached to the back of the bag. The front and flap are embellished with knitted detailing and contrasting whipstitching on the flap edge. If that's not enough, add gold collar buttons and O-rings for just the right glitz. Charlotte's Web is perfect for day and evening, business or pleasure—a major crowd pleaser in any circle.

TITLE: Pretty in Pink
STUDENT: Michelle Hinz
PATTERN: Agenda Book

What woman wouldn't want to have this hot-pink suede agenda book with contrasting perforated black lamb-skin and contrasting black stitching? The book features a magnetic snap for easy access and a larger tab to show off the perforated lambskin. Use the detailing for a coordinated duffel, and you will have a coordinated collection fit for anyone who loves pink!

TITLE: Mega Metallica
STUDENT: Melissa Porcello
PATTERN: Agenda Book

An agenda book doesn't have to be basic or drab. Case in point, check out this one. This book is made of silvery-flecked black leather lined in solid black calfskin leather with contrasting pink stitching. The tab is larger than the original pattern and is attached to the book with two magnetic snaps. Simple and sophisticated, this agenda book is sure to be the perfect gift for that certain someone on your list.

TITLE: Seeing Spots
STUDENT: Amanda Timian
PATTERNS: Hobo Bag and Cell Phone Holder

Don't be confused by this collection and think that there's something wrong with your eyes. You're all right. You're just seeing spots! Gray perforated suede (spots) along with grosgrain polka-dotted ribbon (more spots) coordinate to create a highly sensational collection of spotted accessories. The cell phone holder has been covered in spots with grosgrain ribbon appliqué trim and perforated suede. You can carry the cell phone holder by its oversized handle or attach it to your bag with the dog leash attachment. The hobo bag has a geometric pattern to its gray perforated suede and grosgrain ribbon appliqué trim. You're sure to be noticed any time you're wearing this collection.

TITLE: The Paris Hilton Bag
STUDENT: Kari Mason
PATTERN: Tote Bag

All decked out in your finest attire and nothing to put your personals into? Fear not, oh gracious queen, for we have the perfect bag for you. The Paris Hilton tote bag features embossed leather to resemble the reptiles of the Nile, embellished with a necklace made of rhinestones that looks even better on the bag than it does around the neck. Contrasting handles and bottom add an imperial touch to this perfect accessory. The Paris Hilton bag is not just about the exterior but also the interior, which features a retro print of 1940s ladies in their very best. This bag is sure to turn heads wherever you go.

TITLE: Out of the Louvre
STUDENT: Tracy Vanderbeck
PATTERN: Hobo Bag

Art doesn't always have to be hung on the wall or admired from afar. This hobo bag features a distressed-calf body and lamb-suede handle treatment, with hand-painted detailing and appliqué inlay of your favorite artists. It's a work of art made to be carried and appreciated up close and very *personnel*, as they say in France.

TITLE: On the Go
STUDENT: Ilan Schwarz
PATTERNS: Duffel Bag, Hobo Bag, and Agenda Book

Brown pleated leather with royal blue/light blue suede striping has all the earmarks of a person on the go. Each bag features pleated detailing, along with highlighted suede racing stripes accented with tan piping to bring out the stripe. The hobo bag has metal hardware accents, whereas the duffel features a "constricted" twist to the handle made from an additional tab of leather and attached with a magnetic snap. The agenda book is trim, neat, and highly functional, featuring all the same characteristics as the other two bags. Each bag is unique unto itself, but by adding the agenda book to the mix, you create an ensemble just right for the "dashing Janes."

TITLE: Vernal Equinox
STUDENT: Lauren Eng
PATTERN: Duffel Bag

Step into fall with this high-fashion duffel bag. The emphasis here is on color and style. This duffel features a russet suede body with green suede accents and black leather handles. A tab closure in black leather with a magnetic snap pulls it all together. As with any fall collection, there needs to be a hint of sparkle and this bag is no different. Gold rivets, D-rings, and a metal zipper pull this bag together. Great for walking through a pile of leaves or just taking in the sights and smells of autumn, this bag is perfect for any setting.

TITLE: Starry, Starry Night
STUDENT: Julie Mennucci
PATTERN: Tote Bag

One can never have too many tote bags, let alone too many with stars. This tote is made of camel leather with hand-cut star appliqués in contrasting colors. Check out the inside of this tote, because it also sports a constellation of stars on the inside wall pocket. The bottom of the bag is designed to match the stars and coordinate with the underside of the handles. This stellar tote will illuminate any woman's day or evening wardrobe.

TITLE: Kitty Couture
STUDENT: Terry Tsipouras
PATTERN: Hobo Bag

Nothing says sophistication like fur and sparkling gems, and this hobo bag is no exception. Made of embossed braided lambskin with fur accents, this bag is true to its name. And, it's all about details. Take a close look at the elongated tab made of patent leather and trimmed in rhinestones, the zipper is also trimmed in rhinestones, and, of course, the oversized O-rings to attach the extra-long shoulder strap. Kitty Couture shines, whether you're using this bag for a night on the town or a day in the asphalt jungle.

TITLE: Flower Power
STUDENT: Megan Fishwick
PATTERN: Tote Bag

Tiptoe through the flowers in style with this gray perforated-suede tote, featuring contrasting colored leather handles and handmade leather flower with button accent. For a smooth transition, the handles have been sewn into the body of the bag, rather than being attached with grommets or rivets.

TITLE: Long Live the Queen
STUDENT: Sahra Hussain
PATTERNS: Hobo Bag and Eyeglasses Case

Alice in Wonderland has nothing on our queen. Here she is, the center of attention on an outside pocket, perfect for holding extra items only royalty needs. The front of the hobo is made from one piece of embossed leather, with a quilted stitched pattern and studded with metallic hearts. If we're pulling out all the regal stops, let's continue, because this bag features an appliquéd "card motif," Chanel woven handle technique and metallic-heart zipper pulls.

Her Highness's accessory collection would not be complete without a coordinated eyeglasses case also made of embossed and quilted leather, sporting an appliquéd heart closure with gold studs and accented with a lipstick-red leather binding. May this queen live long and prosper!

TITLE: Ziggy Stardust Goes to the Moon
STUDENT: Kristina Mazurkiewicz
PATTERN: Duffel Bag

A duffel is a duffel: No matter what the size, it still has that same barrel shape. However, when you look at this Glitz and Glam creation, duffel is the last thing you see! Made of silver metallic leather, this duffel has an outside pocket fitted nicely with a metallic zipper on a black fabric background, pink detail stitching throughout the body of the bag, and chains, chains, and more chains! The chain handle is asymmetrical and the detailing chain can be moved, depending on your mood, by a modified dog leash clasp. Also, let's not forget about the extra outside pocket on one side with O-ring and flap closure perfect for your cell phone or other important astrophysical accessories.

TITLE: Reptilian Splendor
STUDENT: Megan Harrington
PATTERN: Agenda Book and Eyeglasses Case

Ideal for anyone, this coordinated set of agenda book and eyeglasses case is sure to make a hit with any big-game hunter. The agenda book features patent embossed leather with hand-painted detailing on black leather appliqué and magnetic snap closure. Inside you'll find a cardholder and assorted pockets modified from the original pattern. The eyeglasses case has the same patent embossed leather with contrasting black leather tab and appliqué. For those who like to keep things real, check out the rugged, raw-edge treatment for a more back-to-nature feel.

TITLE: Going Native
STUDENT: David J. Richardson
PATTERN: Belt and Belt Bag

Perhaps the most useful of all accessories is the belt bag. This one not only has style but sophistication as well. Made of tan leather and trimmed with brown embossed leather, the belt has a metal closure and is styled like a sash. The bag is asymmetrical in shape, with oversized loops that attach the bag to the belt. Rabbit fur screened to look like leopard finishes the look, which is totally jungle boogie! So, get down and go native with this accessory!

SECTION FOUR

 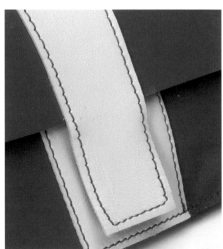 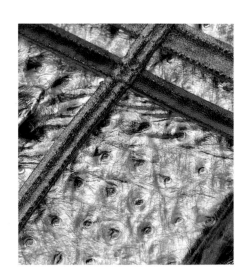

patterns

  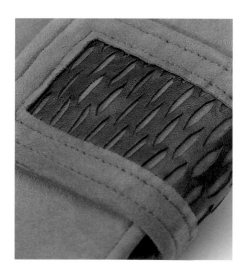

Tote Bag Front and Back Pellon

½ Pattern—Place on fold

Cut 2: Pellon

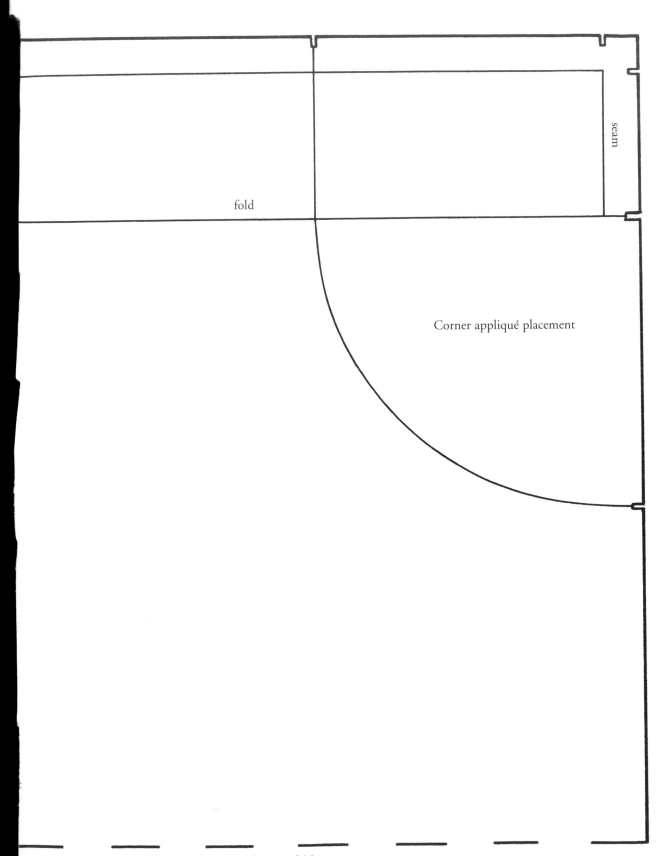

½ Pattern

leather

Rivet hole ●

Fold

Rivet hole ●

seam

fold

Corner appliqué placement

½ Pattern

½ Pattern—Place on fold

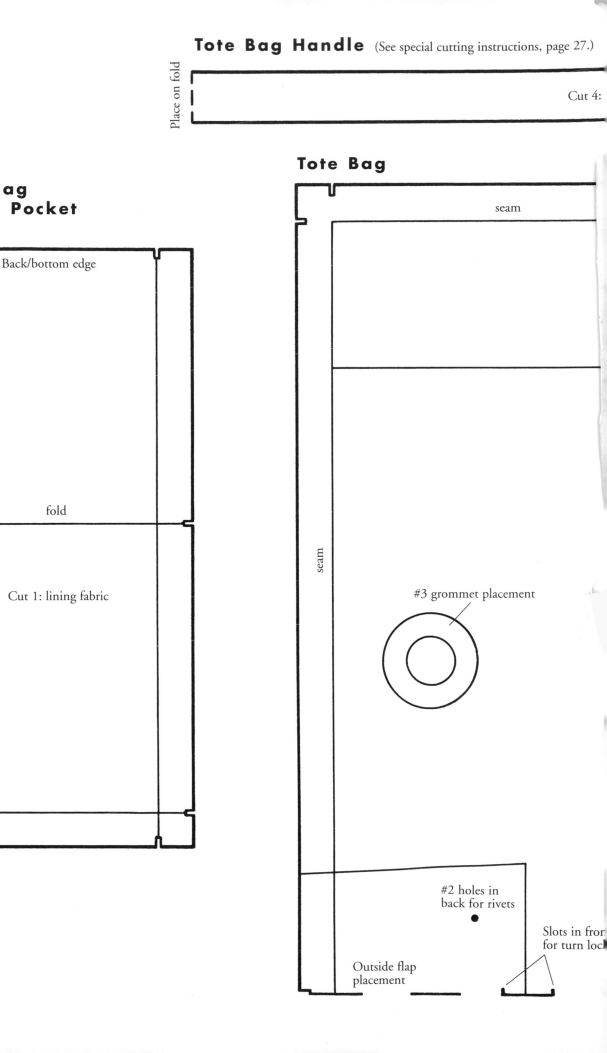

Tote Bag Handle (See special cutting instructions, page 27.)

Place on fold

Cut 4:

Tote Bag

seam

Tote Bag
Lining Pocket

Back/bottom edge

½ Pattern—Place on fold

fold

Cut 1: lining fabric

seam

#3 grommet placement

#2 holes in
back for rivets

Slots in fror
for turn loc

Outside flap
placement

Tote Bag
Outside Bottom

Cut 1: outside leather

¹/₂ Pattern—Place on fold

Tote Bag Lining Collar

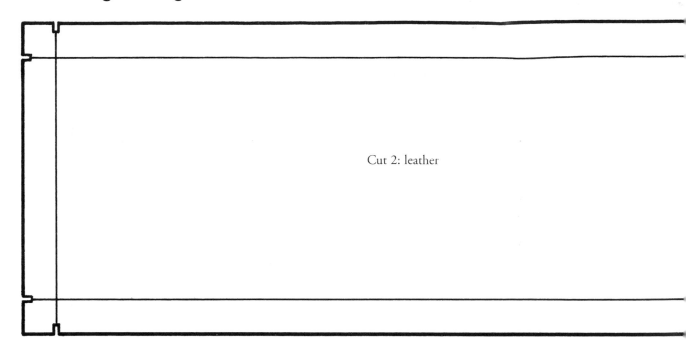

Cut 2: leather

Envelope Bag Front

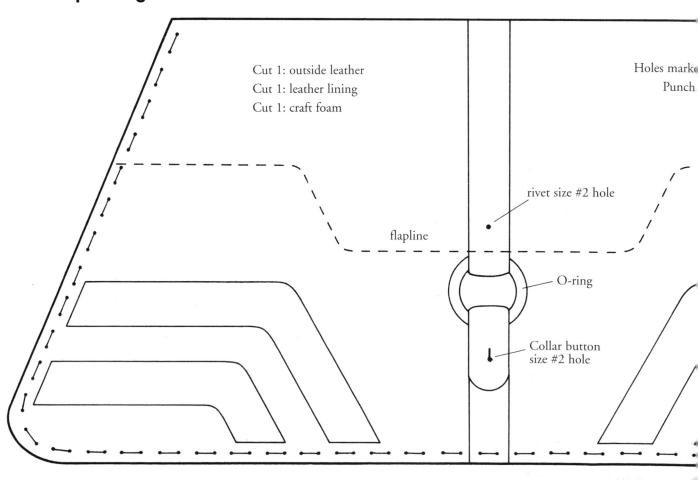

Cut 1: outside leather
Cut 1: leather lining
Cut 1: craft foam

Holes mark
Punch

flapline

rivet size #2 hole

O-ring

Collar button
size #2 hole

Tote Bag Outside Flap

(See special cutting instructions, page 27.)

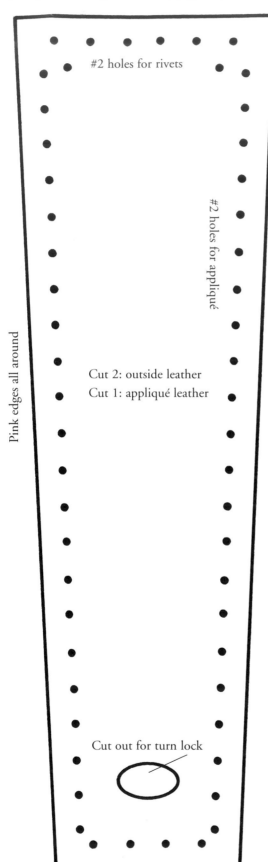

#2 holes for rivets

#2 holes for appliqué

Pink edges all around

Cut 2: outside leather

Cut 1: appliqué leather

Cut out for turn lock

Tote Bag
Bottom Stiffener

½ Pattern—Place on fold

Cut 1: stiffener felt

Tote Bag Lining Front and Back

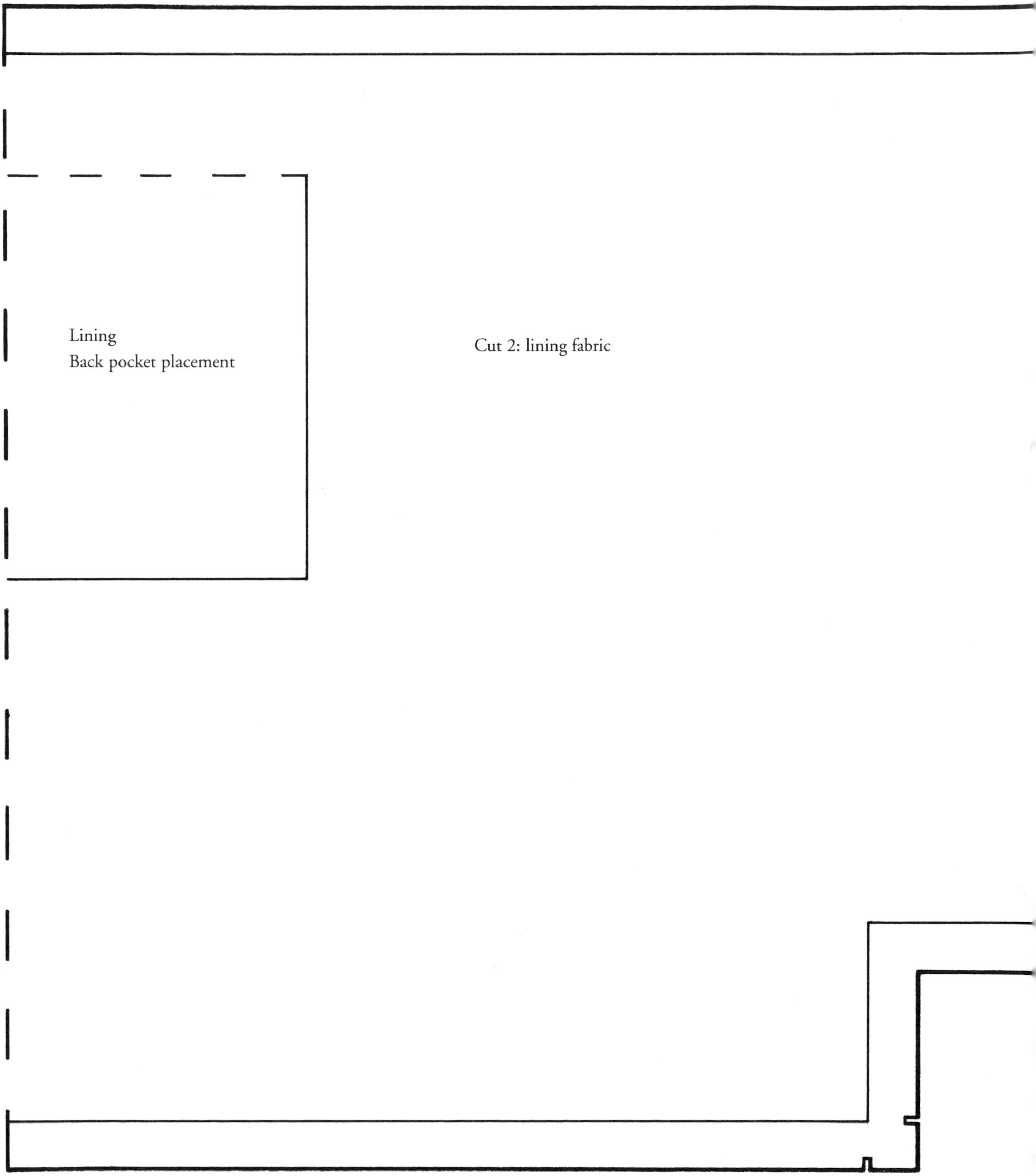

Lining
Back pocket placement

Cut 2: lining fabric

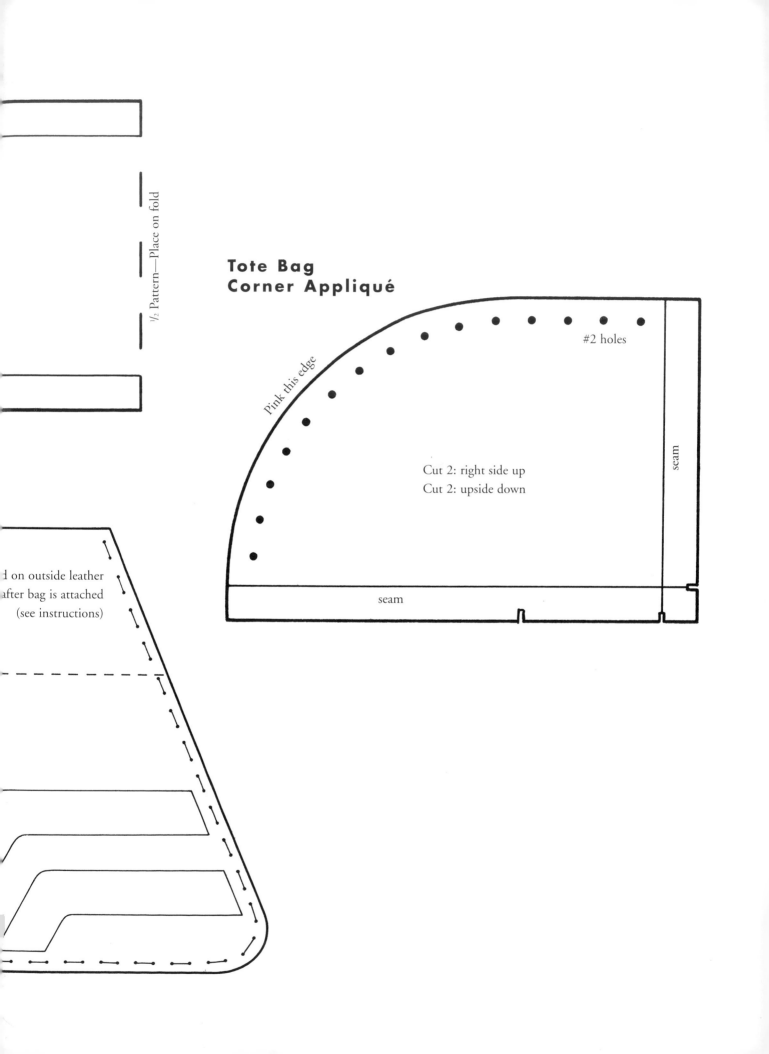

½ Pattern—Place on fold

Tote Bag
Corner Appliqué

Pink this edge

#2 holes

Cut 2: right side up
Cut 2: upside down

seam

seam

d on outside leather
after bag is attached
(see instructions)

Envelope Bag Bottom

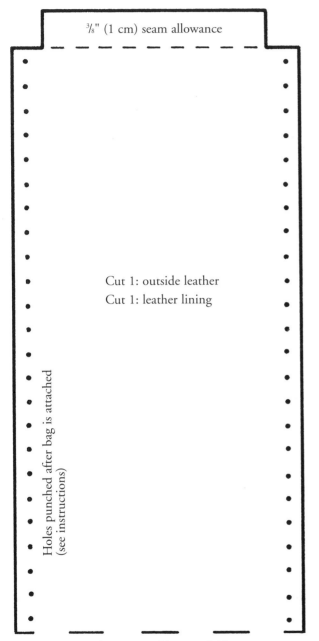

³⁄₈" (1 cm) seam allowance

Cut 1: outside leather
Cut 1: leather lining

Holes punched after bag is attached
(see instructions)

¹⁄₂ Pattern—Place on fold

Envelope Bag
Tab for Handle

(see special cutting instructions)

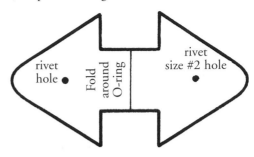

rivet
hole

rivet
size #2 hole

Fold
around
O-ring

Cut 2: snakeskin
Cut 2: outside leather

Envelope Bag
Corner trim #1

Envelope Bag
Corner trim #2

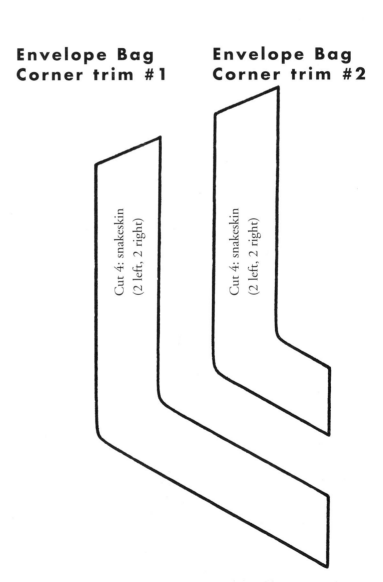

Cut 4: snakeskin
(2 left, 2 right)

Cut 4: snakeskin
(2 left, 2 right)

Envelope Bag
Back Flap Tab

(see special cutting instructions)

rivet

Fold
around
O-ring

stitching
line

Cut 1: snakeskin
Cut 1: outside leather

extend 9"
(22.9 cm)

Envelope Bag
Handle Pattern

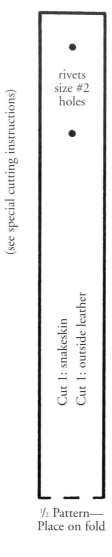

(see special cutting instructions)

rivets
size #2
holes

Cut 1: snakeskin
Cut 1: outside leather

½ Pattern—
Place on fold

Envelope Bag
Front Tab

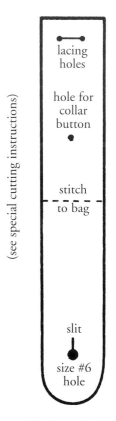

(see special cutting instructions)

lacing
holes

hole for
collar
button

stitch
to bag

slit

size #6
hole

Cut 2: snakeskin

Cut 1: outside leather

Hobo Bag Lining Pattern

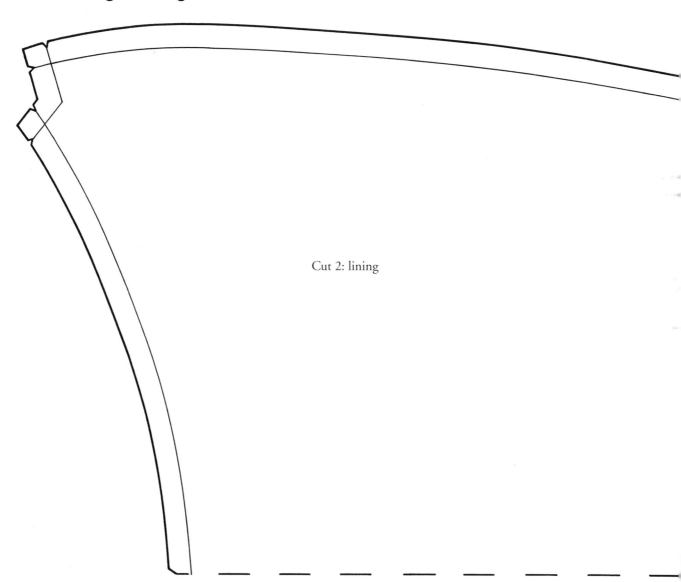

Cut 2: lining

½ Pattern—Place on fold

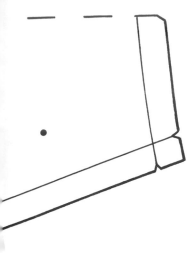

tern

All other holes are eyelets

#2 holes for rivets

Cut 1: outside leather

Hobo Bag Center panel

½ Pattern—Place on fold

Cut 2: outside leather

eyelet holes

Hobo Bag Handle Pat

½ Pattern—Place on fold

Hobo Bag Outside Tab

— slit —

Cut 2: outside leather

— slit —

Tab lining placement

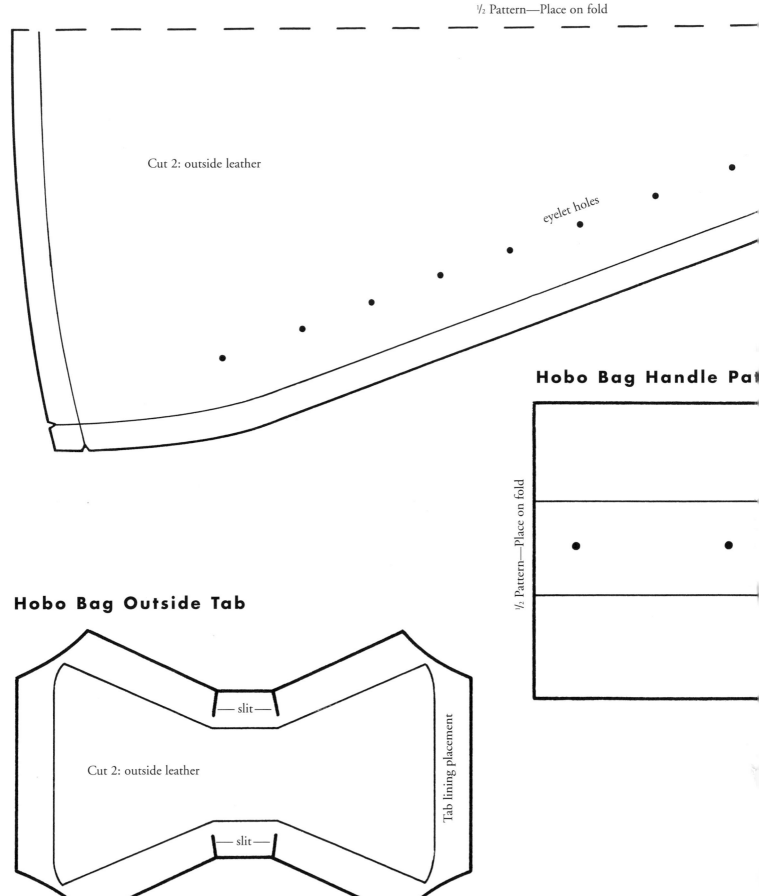

Hobo Bag Tab Lining

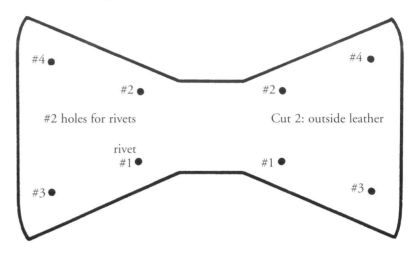

#4 ●   #4 ●

#2 ●   #2 ●

#2 holes for rivets   Cut 2: outside leather

rivet
#1 ●   #1 ●

#3 ●   #3 ●

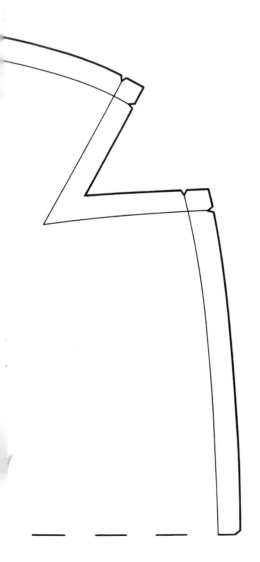

Envelope Bag Gusset (side)

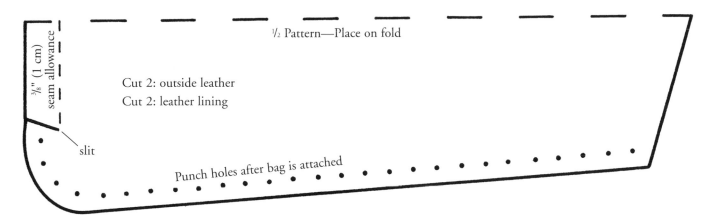

³/₈" (1 cm) seam allowance

½ Pattern—Place on fold

Cut 2: outside leather
Cut 2: leather lining

slit

Punch holes after bag is attached

Envelope Bag Back/Flap

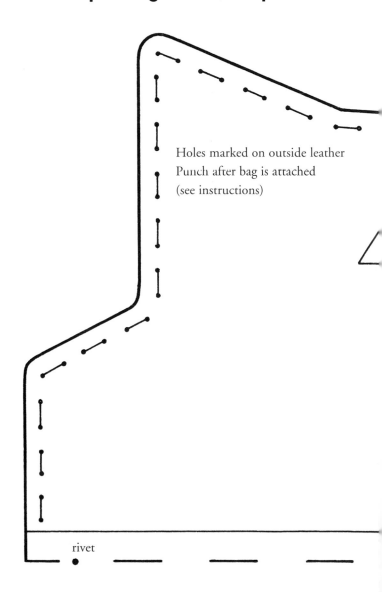

Holes marked on outside leather
Punch after bag is attached
(see instructions)

rivet

Duffel Bag Outside Front/Back

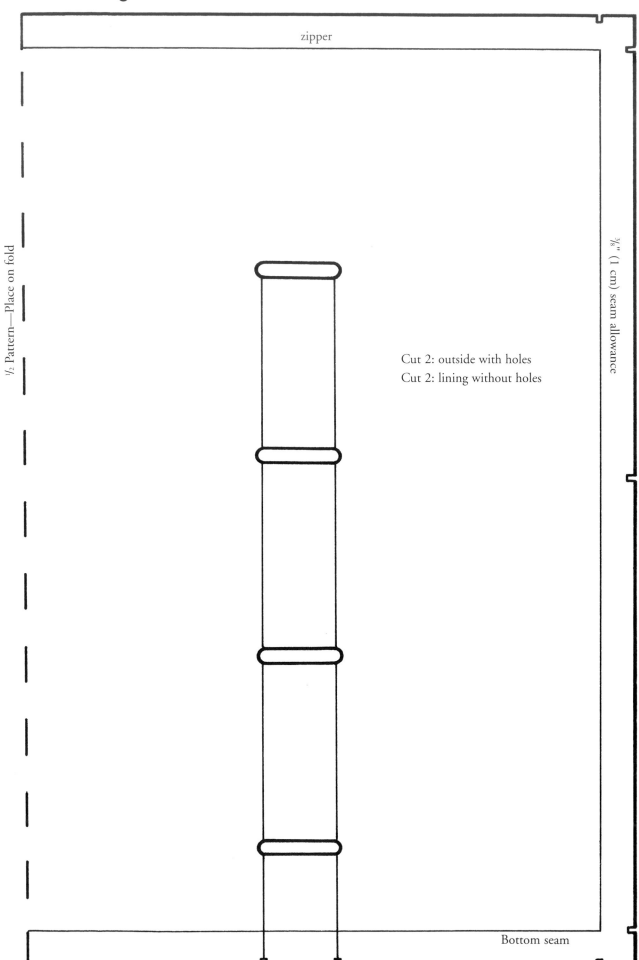

zipper

½ Pattern—Place on fold

⅜" (1 cm) seam allowance

Cut 2: outside with holes
Cut 2: lining without holes

Bottom seam

zipper

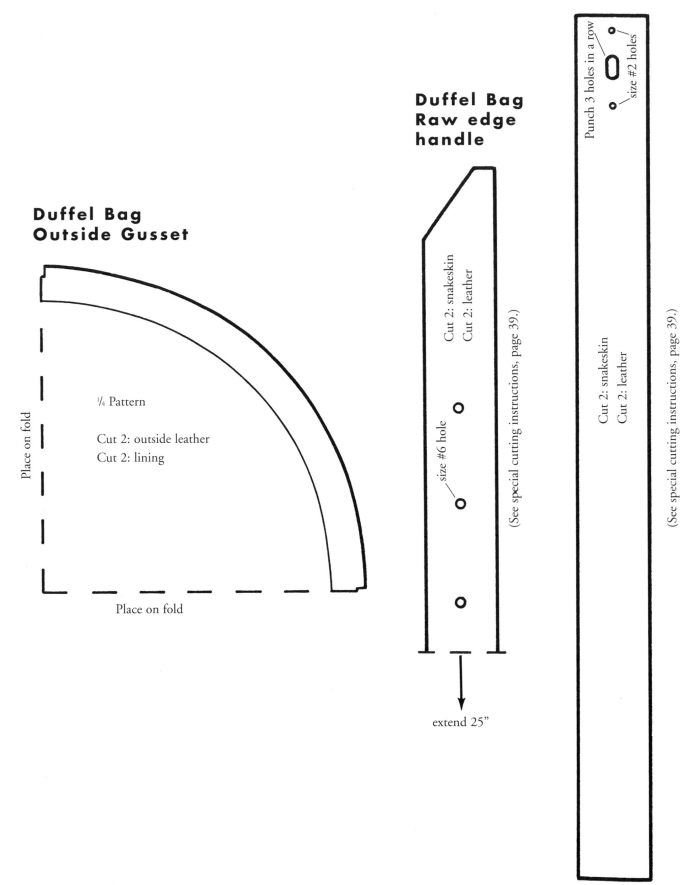

Duffel Bag
Outside Gusset

¼ Pattern

Cut 2: outside leather
Cut 2: lining

Place on fold

Place on fold

Duffel Bag
Raw edge
handle

Cut 2: snakeskin
Cut 2: leather

size #6 hole

(See special cutting instructions, page 39.)

extend 25"

Duffel Bag
Buckle Strap

Punch 3 holes in a row

size #2 holes

Cut 2: snakeskin
Cut 2: leather

(See special cutting instructions, page 39.)

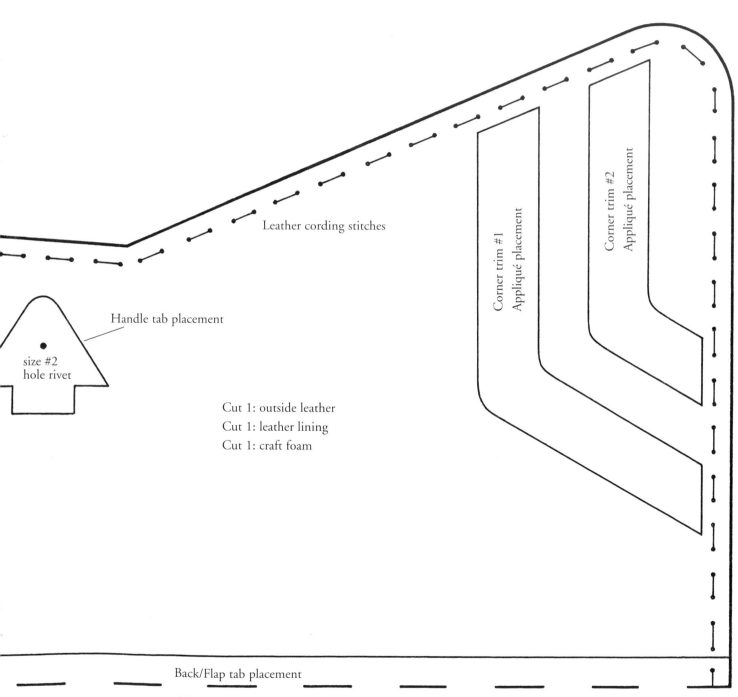

Leather cording stitches

Corner trim #1
Appliqué placement

Corner trim #2
Appliqué placement

Handle tab placement

size #2
hole rivet

Cut 1: outside leather
Cut 1: leather lining
Cut 1: craft foam

Back/Flap tab placement

½ Pattern—Place on fold

Hobo Bag Side Panels

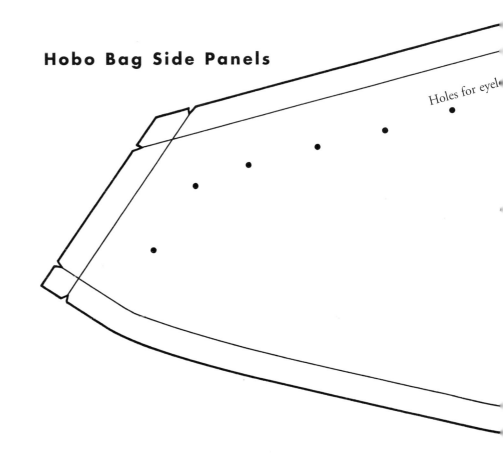

Holes for eyel

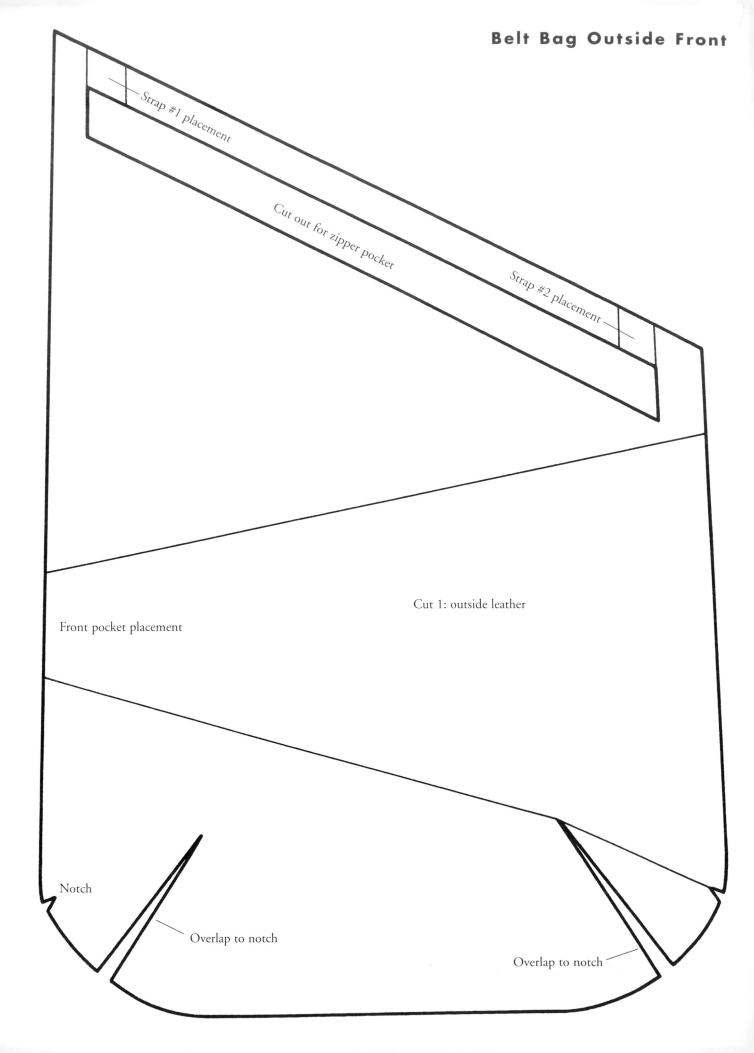

Belt Bag Outside Front

Strap #1 placement

Cut out for zipper pocket

Strap #2 placement

Front pocket placement

Cut 1: outside leather

Notch

Overlap to notch

Overlap to notch

Belt Bag—Outside Back

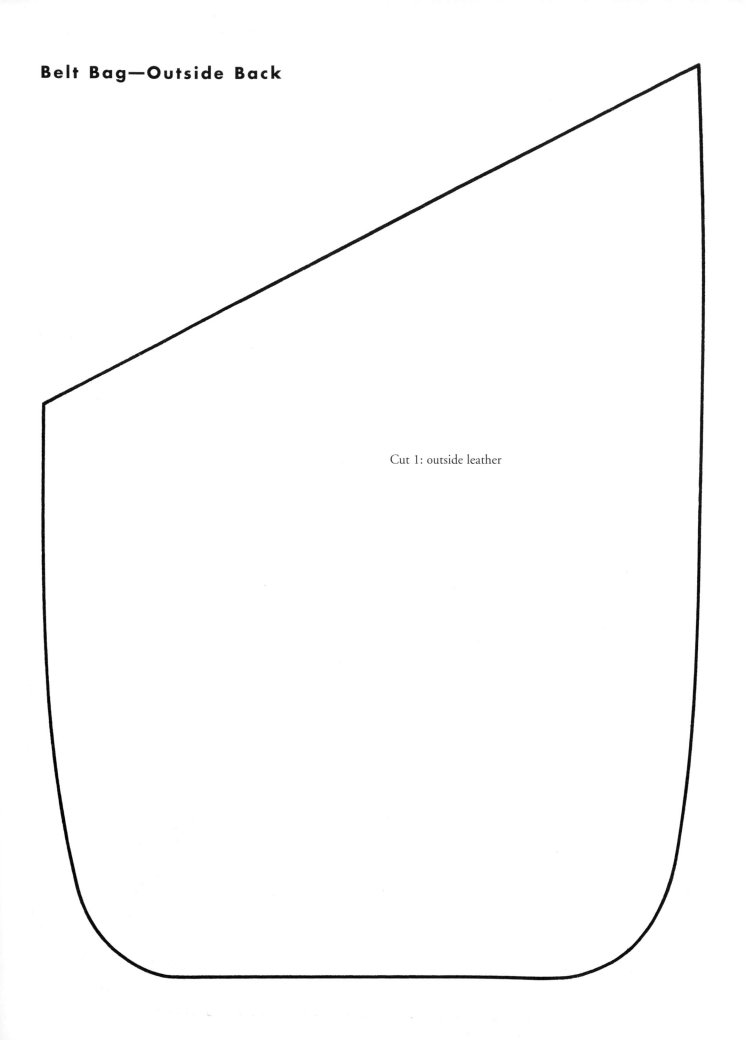

Cut 1: outside leather

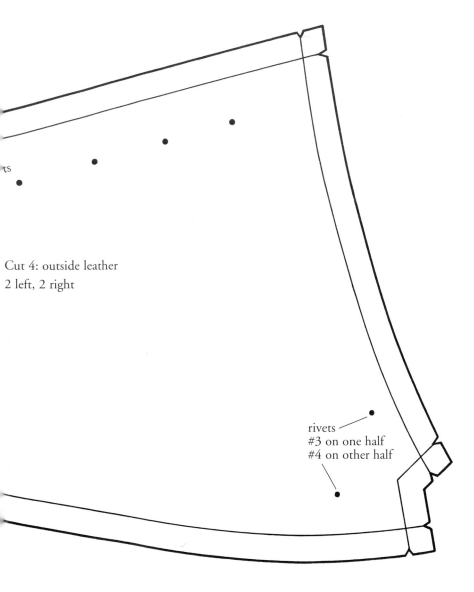

ts

Cut 4: outside leather
2 left, 2 right

rivets
#3 on one half
#4 on other half

Belt Bag Front Pocket

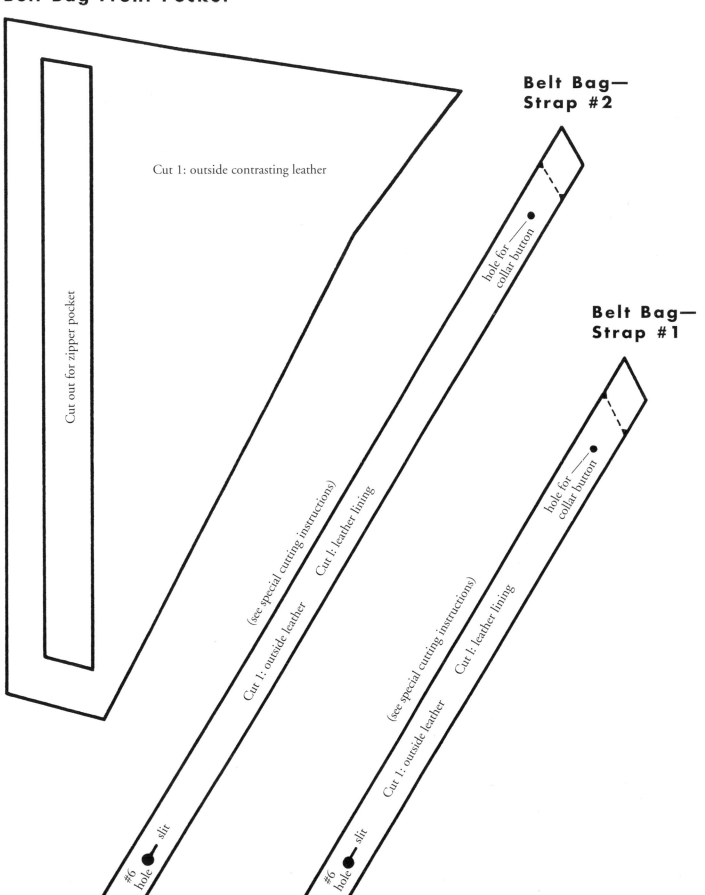

Cut 1: outside contrasting leather

Cut out for zipper pocket

Belt Bag— Strap #2

hole for collar button

(see special cutting instructions)

Cut l: leather lining

Cut 1: outside leather

#6 hole

slit

Belt Bag— Strap #1

hole for collar button

(see special cutting instructions)

Cut l: leather lining

Cut 1: outside leather

#6 hole

slit

Belt for Belt Bag—
Left end

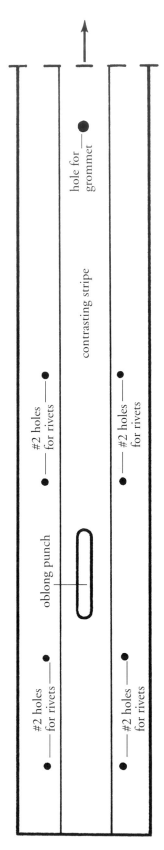

hole for
grommet

contrasting stripe

#2 holes
for rivets

#2 holes
for rivets

oblong punch

#2 holes
for rivets

#2 holes
for rivets

Cut 1: outside leather

Cut 1: leather lining

Stripe for Belt

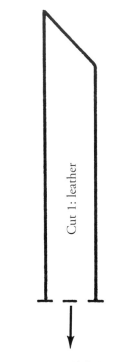

Cut 1: leather

Continue to 36 ⅝" (93 cm)

Keeper for Belt

Cut 1: leather lining

Cut 1: outside leather

(see special cutting instructions)

Belt for Belt Bag— Right end

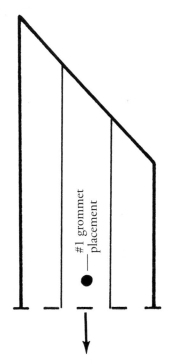

#1 grommet placement

extend to left end
with 14 grommet holes
2" (5.1 cm) apart

(total finished,
16 grommet holes)

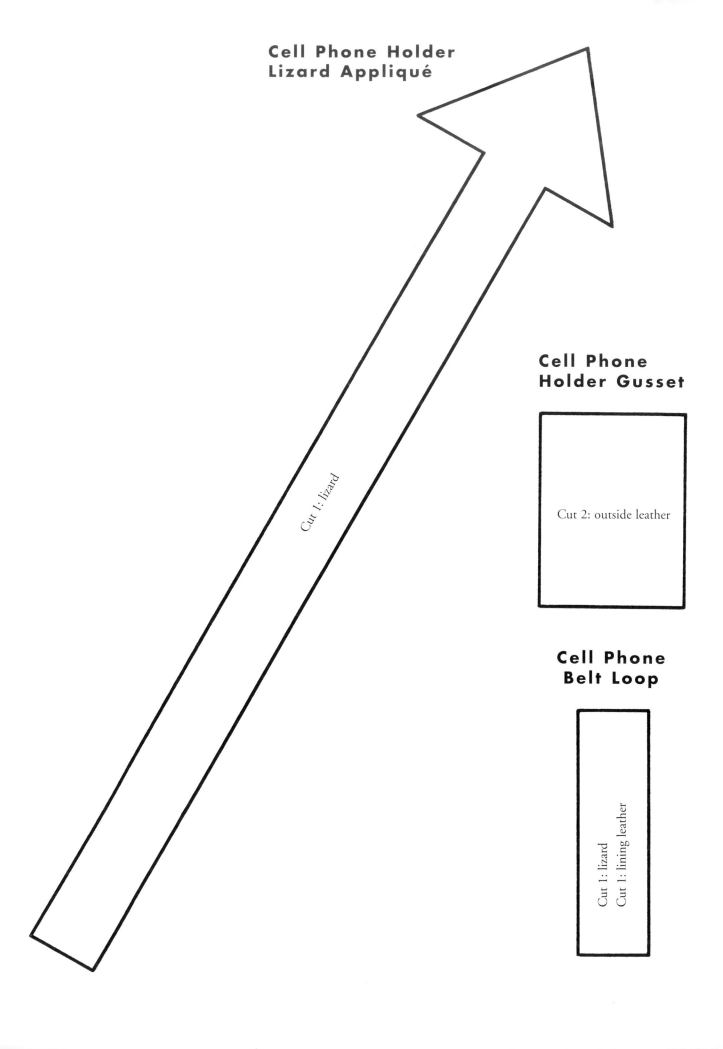

**Cell Phone Holder
Lizard Appliqué**

Cut 1: lizard

Cell Phone Holder Gusset

Cut 2: outside leather

Cell Phone Belt Loop

Cut 1: lizard
Cut 1: lining leather

Cell Phone Holder
gusset placement

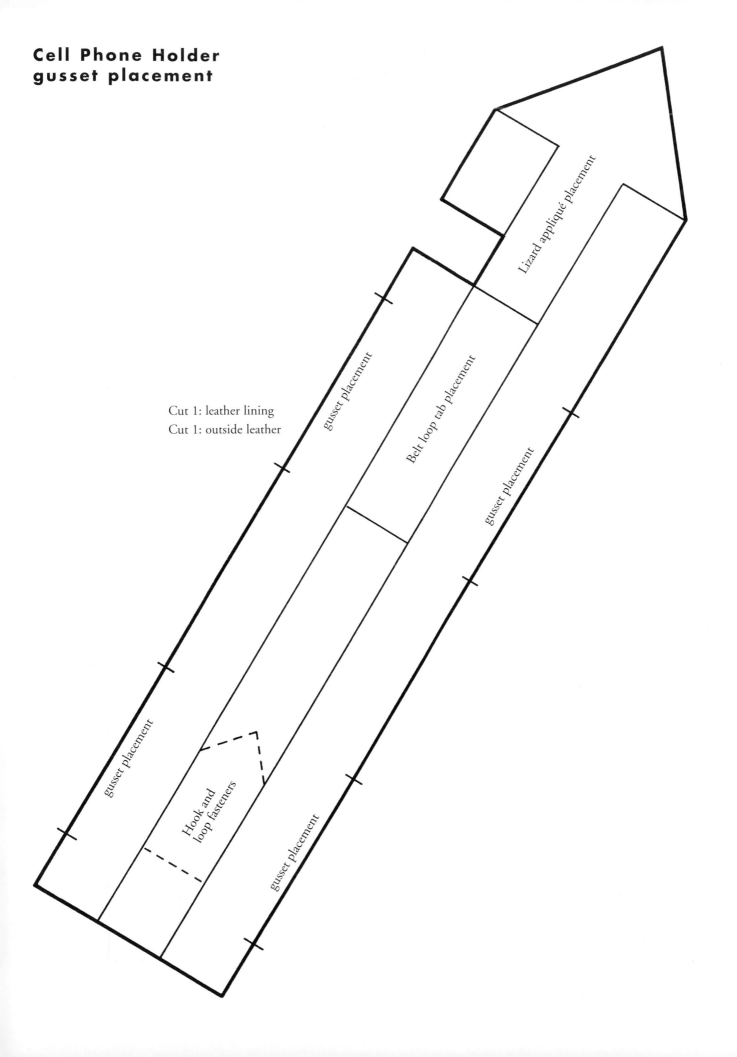

Cut 1: leather lining
Cut 1: outside leather

gusset placement

gusset placement

gusset placement

gusset placement

Belt loop tab placement

Lizard appliqué placement

Hook and
loop fasteners

Cell Phone Holder
Hook and loop placement

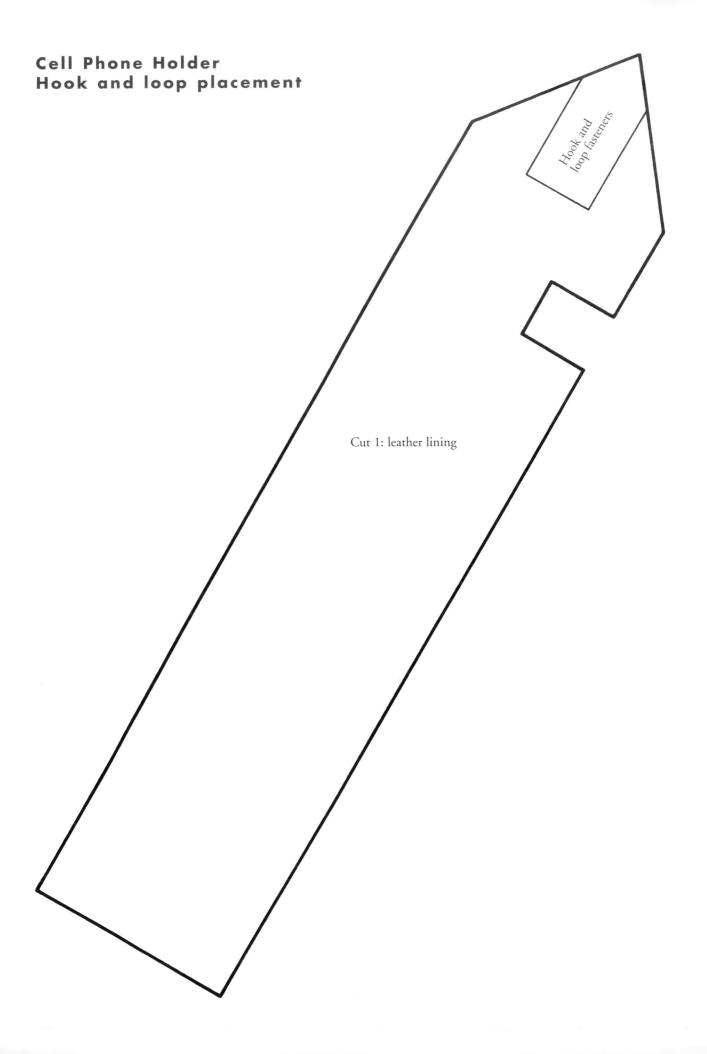

Hook and loop fasteners

Cut 1: leather lining

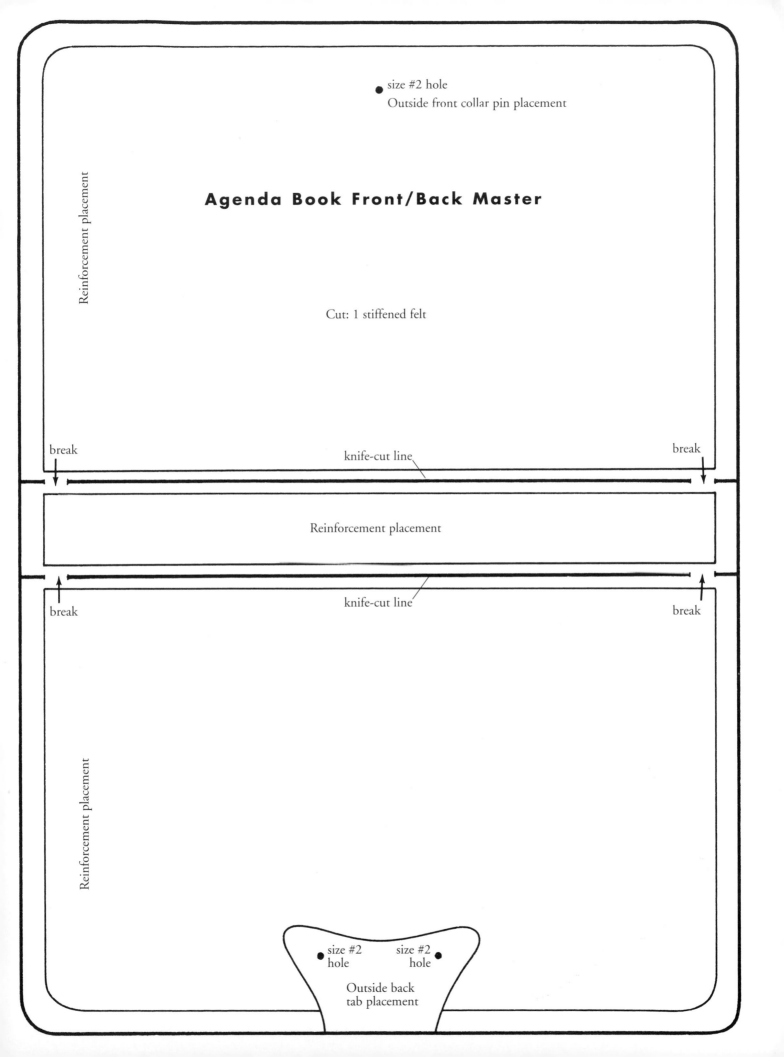

size #2 hole

Outside front collar pin placement

Reinforcement placement

Agenda Book Front/Back Master

Cut: 1 stiffened felt

break

knife-cut line

break

Reinforcement placement

break

knife-cut line

break

Reinforcement placement

size #2
hole

size #2
hole

Outside back
tab placement

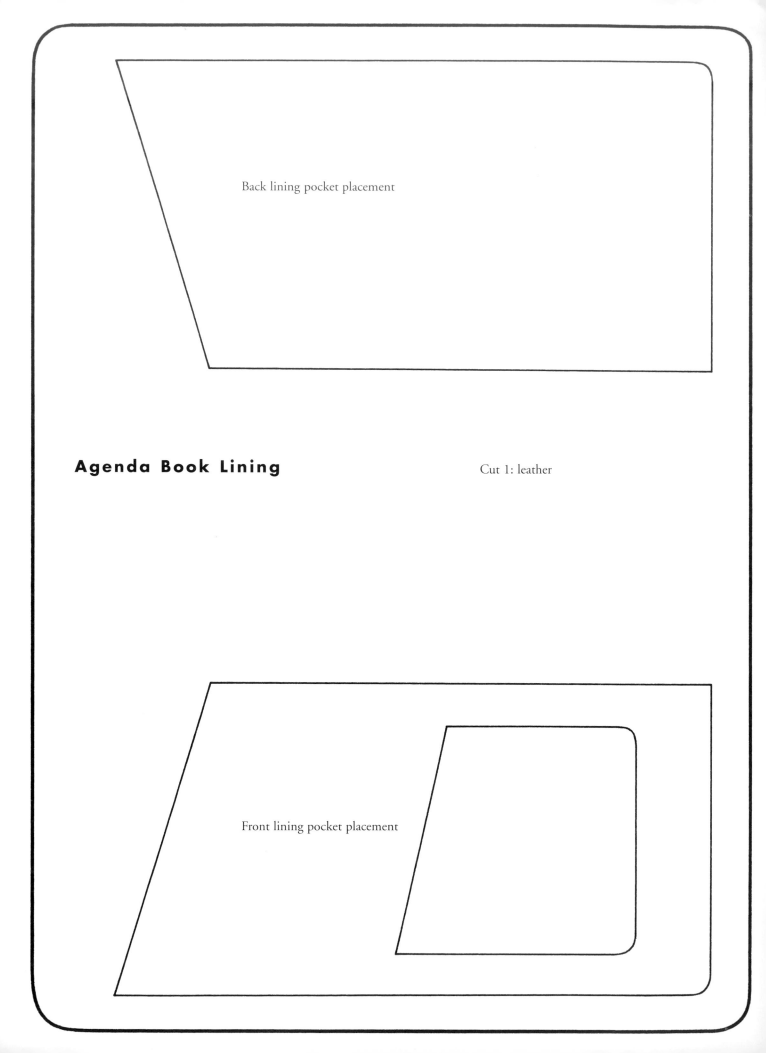

Back lining pocket placement

Agenda Book Lining

Cut 1: leather

Front lining pocket placement

Agenda Book Outside Front and Back

Cut 1: leather

½ Pattern—Place on fold

**Agenda Book
Front/Back Reinforcement**

**Agenda Book
Binding
Reinforcement**

Cut 1: cardboard

Cut 2: cardboard

Agenda Book Outside Tab

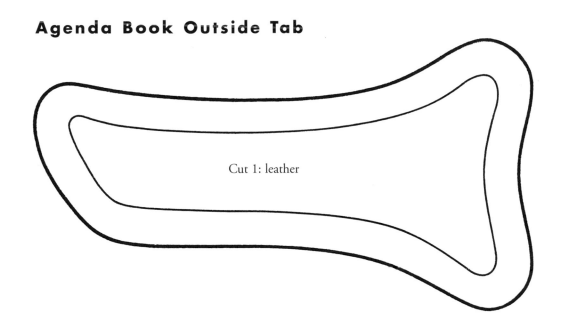

Cut 1: leather

Agenda Book Tab Master

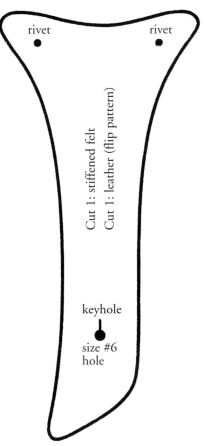

rivet   rivet

Cut 1: stiffened felt
Cut 1: leather (flip pattern)

keyhole

size #6 hole

Agenda Book Lining Card Pocket

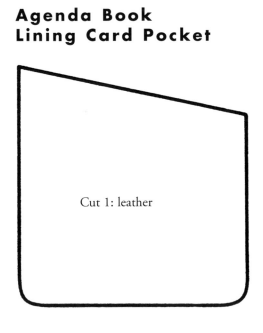

Cut 1: leather

Agenda Book
Lining Pocket

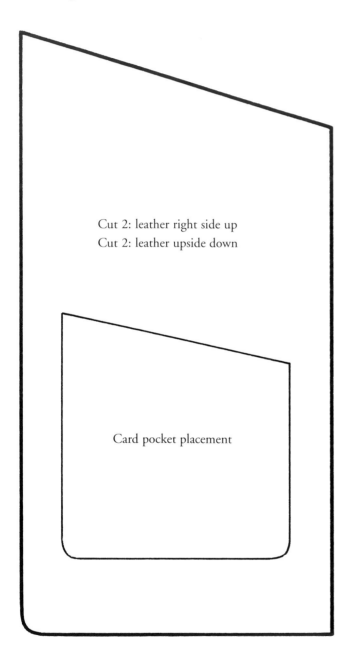

Cut 2: leather right side up
Cut 2: leather upside down

Card pocket placement

Agenda Book
Lining Pocket Interfacing

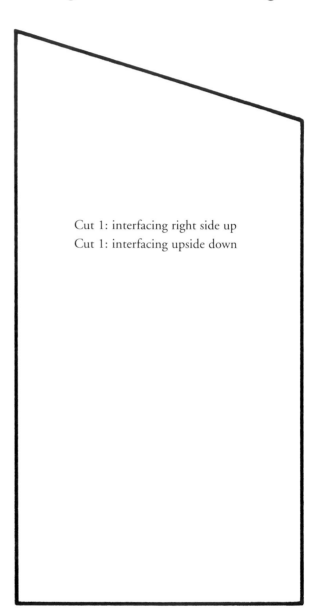

Cut 1: interfacing right side up
Cut 1: interfacing upside down

Eyeglasses Case Front

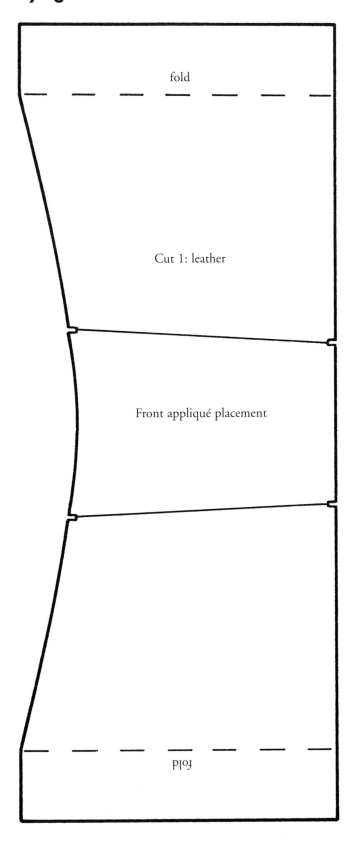

fold

Cut 1: leather

Front appliqué placement

fold

Eyeglasses Case Back and Flap

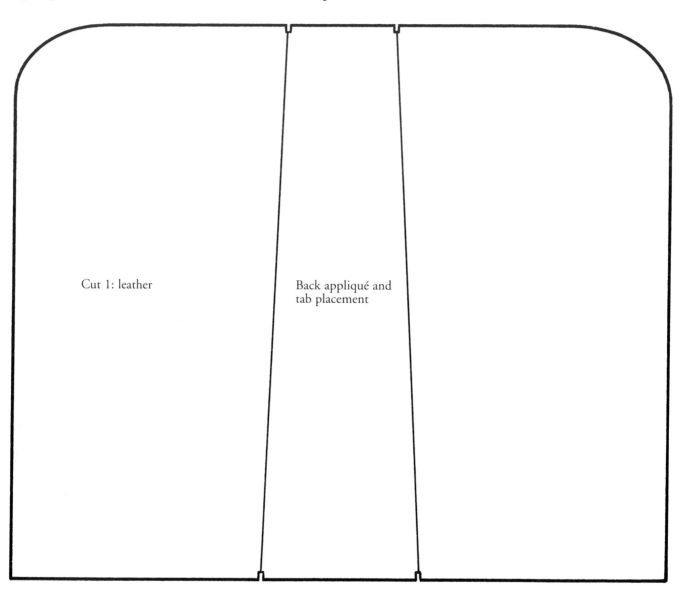

Cut 1: leather

Back appliqué and
tab placement

Eyeglasses Case
Front Appliqué

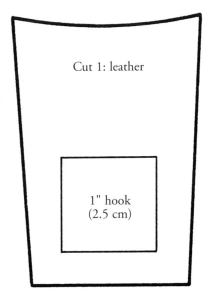

Cut 1: leather

1" hook
(2.5 cm)

Eyeglasses Case Back Appliqué and Tab

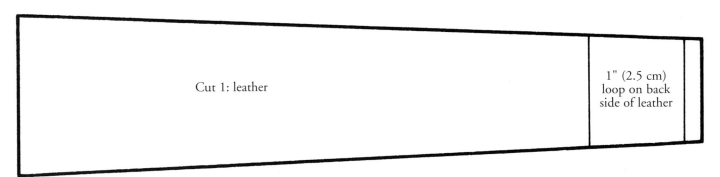

Cut 1: leather

1" (2.5 cm)
loop on back
side of leather

contributors

Lauren Eng
sohoLau83@yahoo.com

Megan Fishwick
megFish@aol.com

Megan Harrington
meggiebabe17@aol.com

Michelle Hinz
designxtc@aol.com

Sahra Hussain
sahra_hussain@hotmail.com

Kari Mason
kashmir674@aol.com

Kristina Mazurkiewicz
periwinks6@aol.com

Julie Mennucci
julsmennuch@hotmail.com

Shelley Parker
inmyshoes@nyc.rr.com

Melissa Porcello
melFIT417@aol.com

Hannah Polgar
hanLnah@aol.com

David J. Richardson
donlywear@aol.com

Ilan Schwarz
ilan2@hotmail.com

Amanda Timian
designsbyajay@yahoo.com

Terry Tsipouras
greekgod122000@yahoo.com

Tracy Vanderbeck
vandergogh4@aol.com

glossary

Appliqué: A cutout decoration fastened to a larger piece of material by sewing or adhesive.

Binder Clip: Also called "bull dog clips," these strong metal clips are sold in stationery or office supply stores for holding large stacks of paper, but they also work well for holding pieces of leather together.

Bone Folder: Originally made of bone but now often made of plastic, this tool is used to open and flatten seams or turn edges when working with leather.

Embossed Leather: Features a pattern on the surface of the hide or skin. Embossing is generally used to simulate other more exotic animal skins such as alligator, ostrich, or crocodile.

Embroidery Needle: A classic needle with an oversized eye used for sewing embroidery stitches on cloth or leather.

Eyelet: A small, circular metal ring that is set into a hole primarily designed to receive a cord or used as decoration.

Gauge Foot: A sewing machine presser foot that has an edge guide, which allows you to stitch a predetermined measurement from the needle.

Glover's Needle: An "arrowhead" shaped, highly sharp, three-sided needle used for beading on leather.

Grommet: A metal eyelet used as decoration or to strengthen and protect an opening. Also used to insulate or protect something passed through it, such as cording or a handle.

Gusset: An insert in the side of a bag to give it depth and expansion.

Hair-on Leather: A type of leather where, during the tanning process, the hair has been left on and finished to simulate pony, zebra, tiger, or other animals.

Hide: The leather from a large animal such as a cow, buffalo, or deer, usually cut in half and sold as sides for handbags and footwear.

Interfacing: A material that is placed between the outside fabric and the lining to add support and strength to the bag.

Lacing Needle: A flat needle with a wedge-type device at the eye for gripping the lace.

Lining: Fabric or lightweight leather used for the inside of the bag. It can be the same color as the outside of the bag or a contrasting color for more visual interest.

Pinking: A V-shaped edge made by using pinking shears to cut a serrated edge at a seam to prevent fabric from raveling. Also used as a decorative edge on fabrics and leathers.

Quilting: The effect obtained by stitching, either by hand or machine, two or more layers of fabric together with padding in between. The stitching can be a geometric pattern or a decorative design.

Reverse Appliqué or Inlay: The ability to add color and shape through cutwork. Contrasting colored leather is placed under the surface leather that has been cut out to resemble a shape, flower, or animal.

Rotary Cutter: A tool with a round blade, resembling a pizza cutter, used for cutting straight lines on fabric.

Silk-screened Leather: A skin that has a printed decorative design motif added to the surface.

Skin: The leather from smaller animals such as calf, goat, pig, and snake. The skin from one animal is usually sold as a full piece.

Smocking: A hand-stitching technique that secures the pleats or folds of the material.

Snakeskin: The skin from a snake that has been tanned and finished.

Suede: A finish that has been added to the hide or skin to create a buffed or brushed surface.

Teflon Foot: A sewing machine presser foot (either made entirely of Teflon or Teflon coated) used to sew leather and suede.

Top Stitching: Decorative stitching used to add detailing to a sewing project. It is often done in a contrasting thread color.

Trapunto: A decorative quilted design in high relief this is worked through at least two layers of cloth or leather by outlining the design in running stitch and padding it from the underside.

Zipper Foot: A single-toed presser foot that is notched on both sides to accommodate the needle and to facilitate stitching a zipper.

resources

A.C. Moore
www.acmoore.com
Nationwide Locations
(Arts and crafts supplies)

Active Trimming Co.
250 West 39th Street
New York, NY 10018 USA
(800) 878–6336
Catalog available

Atlanta Thread & Supply Co.
695 Red Oak Road
Stockbridge, GA 30281 USA
(800) 847–1001
(Notions)
Catalog available

Brewer Sewing Supplies
3800 West 42nd Street
Chicago, IL 60632 USA
(800) 444–3111
(Sewing supplies)

Charm Woven Labels
2400 West Magnolia Boulevard
Burbank, CA 91506 USA
(800) 843–1111
www.charmwoven.com
(Woven labels)
Catalog available

The Fabric & Fiber Sourcebook
Published by *Threads Magazine*
Mail-order guideavailable through
Amazon.com and Barnesandnoble.com

Galart International
www.galartintl.com
(Suppliers of exotic leather and
accessories)

Global Leather
253 West 35th Street
New York, NY 10001 USA
(212) 244–5190
(Variety of leathers and suede)

Hansol Sewing Machine Co., Inc.
101 West 26th Street
New York, NY 10001 USA
(800) 463–9661
(Sewing machines)

Herrschners
(800) 441–0838
(Sewing and craft supplies, fabrics)
Catalog available

Hermès Leather
49 West 38th Street
New York, NY 10018 USA
(212) 947–1153 or (888) 947–1159
www.hermesleather.com
(Variety of leathers and suede)

HobbyCraft Canada
(Hobbycraft.com stores nationwide)
(craft supplies)

HobbyCraft Group Limited
7 Enterprise Way
Aviation Park
Bournemouth International Airport
Christchurch
Dorset BH23 6HG UK
01202 596100
www.hobbycraft.co.uk
(Craft supplies)

International Internet Leather Crafter's Guild
http://iilg.org

JoAnn Fabrics
(888) 739–4120
www.joann.com
Nationwide locations
(Craft Supplies, fabrics, and trimmings)
Catalog and magazine available

The Leather Crafters Online Source
www.eleathersupply.com
(877) 433–8468

The Leather Factory
www.leatherfactory.com
Select store locations
(Leathers and suede)

Leather, Suede, Skins, Inc.
261 West 35th Street
New York, NY 10001 USA
(212) 967–6616
www.leathersuedeskins.com
(Variety of leathers and suede)

M & J Trimming
1008 6th Avenue
New York, NY 10018 USA
(212) 391–9072
(Trimmings)

Michael's Arts & Crafts
www.michaels.com
Nationwide locations
(Arts and crafts supplies)

Mr. Hyde's Leather Sales
www.mrhydesleather.com
(Supplier of leathers)

C.S. Osborne Tools
125 Jersey Street
Harrison, NJ 07029 USA
(973) 483–3232
(Tools)
Catalog available

Pearl Paint
www.pearlpaint.com
Nationwide Locations
(Craft supplies)
Catalog available

Siegel of California
www.siegelofca.com
(800) 862–8956
(Leather supplies, tools, and notions)

Tandy Leather & Crafts
(800) 555–3130
www.tandyleather.com
(Crafting tools, leather, and suede)
Catalog available

Universal Mercantile Exchange, Inc.
13200 Brooks Drive #E
Baldwin Park, CA 91706 USA
(800) 921–5523
www.umei.com
(Buckles, buttons, chains, fasteners, handles, ornaments, and trims)
Catalog available

Veteran Leather
36–14 35th Street
Long Island City, NY 11106 USA
(718) 786–9000
(Leather and suede)
Catalog available

Westphal & Co.
105 West 30th Street
New York, NY 10001 USA
(212) 563–5990
(Tools)
Catalog available

about the authors

Ellen Goldstein-Lynch is the chairperson of the accessories design department at the Fashion Institute of Technology, in New York. She is a full professor and the 2003 recipient of the SUNY Chancellors Award for Excellence in Teaching. She has been involved in the accessories field for 25 years. She has served as public relations director for the National Fashion Accessories Association for 10 years. She is an authority on handbags and accessories and has been featured on national television and in print. She is also the author of *The Accessories Bible: A Quick Reference Guide for Accessories Enthusiasts*.

Sarah Mullins is a graduate and faculty member of the accessories design department at the Fashion Institute of Technology. Sarah does freelance design for several New York–based companies and also has her own line of unique handbags. Her passion is experimenting with different combinations of materials in her designs.

Nicole Malone is an accessories designer with a passion for handbags. She has freelance experience in patternmaking, samplemaking, and construction of one-of-a-kind creations for various handbag and fashion designers. A graduate of the accessories design program at the Fashion Institute of Technology, she currently designs and produces her own line of handbags and belts, but her true love is teaching in the accessories department at her alma mater.

They are also coauthors of *Making Handbags: Retro, Chic, Luxurious* (Rockport Publishers, 2002).

acknowledgments

Ellen Goldstein-Lynch

To Jim, Thomas, Janis, Little Brandon, Larry, Jess, and Hoolie, you guys totally "light up my life!" Thanks for your dedication, love, and support. To my son Brandon, my light, my inspiration, I will cherish you forever. To Gale Keenan, "buds forever." To my brother Dennis, once lost now found. Special kudos to the dynamic group of students, faculty, and friends with whom I share my life at FIT.

Thanks to Mary Ann and the Rockport crew for pitching this book and the first one to us. To Nicole and Sarah, thanks for letting me be as creative as you guys. It was totally amazing! And to Drs. John Marino and Elisa Port; without you, I would not be here today!!!

Sarah Mullins

I would like to thank Alex, my family and friends for their support and encouragement. Thank you, Maureen, for testing all my prototypes; you wear them well. To the faculty, staff, and students of the FIT accessories design department, you all make learning exciting. Thank you to Nicole, who speaks the same handbag language, and to Ellen and Mary Ann for repeating a great book-writing experience.

Nicole Malone

To my former instructors and present-day colleagues at FIT who have taught me so much over the years—and still do to this day. To all of my talented students who make me love what I do! To Sarah (for keeping me sane), Ellen (for your encouragement), Mary Ann and all of the wonderful people at Rockport Publishers for making this book possible. To my friends for always being there for me (especially Shelley and Brian). To my entire family (especially Mom and Dad); I never forget how lucky I am to have you! To Kevin, my love always, and of course, my Shooky!